PRAISE FOR *WAKING UP IN THE WILDERNESS*

"Natalie Ogbourne is a long-standing citizen of the Yellowstone Nation, and in *Waking Up in the Wilderness* she chronicles the richly rewarding arts, skills, and wisdoms she has earned in many seasons of watching "Yellowstone being Yellowstone." Her enthusiastic and affable tales of exploring the park display not only good sense but an admirable humility in the face of Yellowstone's wonders."

–Paul Schullery, author of *Mountain Time, Searching for Yellowstone: Ecology and Wonder in the Last Wilderness,* and *The Bear Doesn't Know: Life and Wonder in Bear Country.*

"Natalie Ogbourne's *Waking Up in the Wilderness* takes us on adventures where the epic wild majesty of Yellowstone National Park is as much a character as Ogbourne and her family. From the bison and bear that prowl the landscape, to the trails threaded through deep pinewoods, to the author's beloved Old Faithful Inn where her journeys in this magic place first began, this account of Ogbourne's repeated pilgrimages to Yellowstone illuminates a place where the wilderness and civilization interact in a very intimate and strange way, like the dynamic landscape in Yellowstone itself. Through this lens of forays into this special place, Ogbourne shows readers the mercies of nature, love, passing time, and family."

—Nicholas Trandahl, award-winning poet, author of *Mountain Song* and *Purgatory*

"This book is as close as possible to experiencing the beauty and grandeur of Yellowstone without being there. Through Natalie's words and descriptions, the reader can almost hear the thundering waters cascading over the Upper Falls of the Yellowstone River or feel the stream of hot water gushing upwards from Old Faithful Geyser. *Waking Up in the Wilderness* brought back precious memories of my own visits to Yellowstone National Park."

—Paul Stutzman, author of *Hiking Through: One Man's Journey to Peace and Freedom on the Appalachian Trail*

WAKING UP IN THE WILDERNESS

WAKING UP IN THE WILDERNESS

A YELLOWSTONE JOURNEY

NATALIE OGBOURNE

Copyright © 2024 by Natalie Ogbourne

All rights reserved.

No part of this book may be reproduced in any form or by any electronic or mechanical means, including information storage and retrieval systems, without written permission from the author, except for the use of brief quotations in a book review.

A disclaimer of sorts: This is a work of non-fiction, which means it's true. This particular work of non-fiction falls under the genre of memoir which, by definition, is based on memory. In this case, the memory is mine, which means the stories and conversations surrounding the events have been rendered as I recall them. While my editor suggested I was too hard on myself and my husband said I was too kind to him, this is how I remember things. Memory is a matter of perspective.

ISBN Number: 979-8-9913761-0-5

Cover Designer: Kaeley Dunteman-Stiefvater | wilderlovewisco.com

Cover Photo: Jaime Ogbourne

Map: BMR Williams | bmrwilliams.com

Oak Stream Odysseys

Dedicated to

*Mom and Dad,
who first took me to Yellowstone,*

*Mason, Elyse, and Emma,
who made going to Yellowstone so much fun,*

*and to Jaime,
who keeps keeping his promise to bring me back.*

Everybody needs beauty as well as bread, places to play in and pray in, where nature may heal and give strength to body and soul alike.

JOHN MUIR, *THE YOSEMITE*

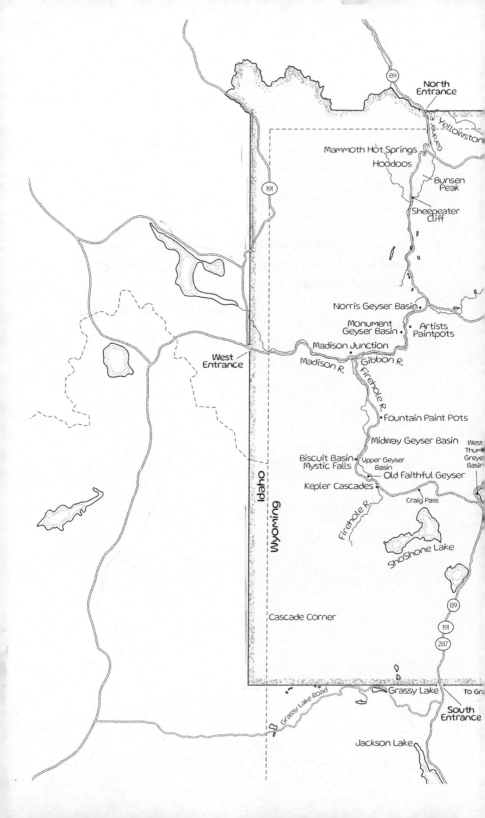

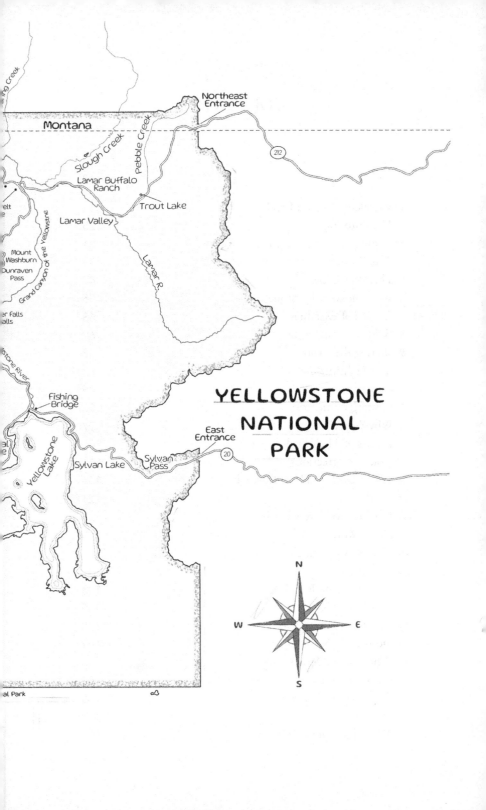

CONTENTS

Prologue	15
1. Miscalculation or Miracle	19
2. The Entourage	25
3. Waking Up in Yellowstone	31
4. Bear Country	39
5. This Way, Babe	47
6. Welcome to Yellowstone	55
7. A Land of Extremes	63
8. Wild and Dangerous	69
9. Sharing the Road	77
10. Bear-Fighting Stick	83
11. Dangerous Ground	89
12. Pushing Boundaries	93
13. Why Worry?	97
14. Echoes of Their Dad	105
15. Course Corrections	111
16. Taking the Road Less Traveled	115
17. Reading Rivers	121
18. Learning to Throw Feathers	125
19. Don't Worry	135
20. That Wasn't in the Forecast	141
21. Hiking In	147
22. Lamar Buffalo Ranch	153
23. Worth the Wait	159
24. Bear Frequenting Area	165
25. Do-Overs	169
26. What the Wilderness Does	175
27. Oceans of Snow	181
28. A Season for Everything	185
29. Priorities	193
30. The Weight of the Wilderness	197

31. No Guarantee	207
32. It Changes Everything	215
Epilogue	223
Resources and Reading	225
Acknowledgements	227
Also By Natalie Ogbourne	229
About the Author	231

PROLOGUE

Sixty thousand miles. It's a staggering number. At least it was for me.

I'd just added the last two trips to the list of visits I'd made to Yellowstone during my lifetime. There were thirty of them. I'm not a math person, but one of those dreaded word problems started to assemble itself in my head: Natalie lives in Iowa. Yellowstone is a thousand miles from Iowa. If Natalie travels to Yellowstone thirty times in forty-four years, how many highway miles will she have logged getting there and back again?

Like I said, sixty thousand is a staggering number—especially to a single destination. But it wasn't just any destination. It was to a national park. And it wasn't just any national park. It was Yellowstone National Park—America's first and my favorite. I've visited sixteen others, several of them repeatedly, and enjoyed every one. But Yellowstone remains the one for me.

Over those forty-four years, I've walked every boardwalk and driven every stretch of public road. What I haven't done is hike every trail. This is mostly because I like to revisit the ones I've hiked before, often because I like what I found at the end of the trail. Not only do I want to see what I saw again, I want to see how it's changed.

I was eighteen, working at the Old Faithful Inn and standing across the counter from a park visitor, when I started to understand the importance of stopping long enough—or often enough—to see. After asking, as was my habit, about my customer's time in the park, I smiled and nodded sympathetically as the man launched into a short-but-passionate tale of woe. It was eight in the morning and he was worn, stressed, and irritable. *On vacation.*

"It's not Yellowstone. This place is great," he said as I placed his items in a bag. "It's this tour my wife has us on. We race from one thing to the next. We never stop long enough to really see."

That conversation was in 1987. That's how long I've been helping people make the most of their time in Yellowstone—people already in the park, people in my life, and even people I've met online. Somewhere along the way, I went from simply helping people know what there is to see and do in Yellowstone to writing and speaking about what I've seen and how it shapes my life.

Waking Up in the Wilderness is more than a story of me and my family doing what we love, in a place we love, with people we love. It's a sign saying "Look at this!" so readers can experience the park and see what there is to see for themselves.

It's said that a journey of a thousand miles begins with a single step. Or perhaps the rotation of a tire. Or even the turn of a page. Let's go to Yellowstone.

YELLOWSTONE NATIONAL PARK

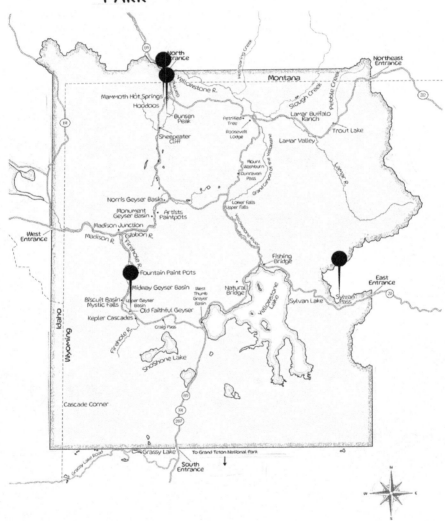

1 MISCALCULATION OR MIRACLE

"Y'all are thirsty," our server drawled as she refilled our glasses in the Mammoth Hotel Dining Room. "You must have been out skiing today."

That we had. An oversnow shuttle had dropped my family—my mom, dad, younger brother Matt, and me—off on the side of the groomed and packed snow road that morning. An eighteen-year-old from the Midwest, I'd never skied. I was not an athlete or even an outdoorsy person. Yet there I was, alone in the wintry woods relying on my family and our skis to make it back to civilization. As I watched the shuttle lumber away from that isolated place, the sound of its retreating motor muffled by January's thick blanket of snow, the weight of the wilderness settled on my soul.

We set off through silent frosted forest, our trail at first following the Gardner River then winding around the base of Bunsen Peak. Propelling across flat open spaces and pushing ourselves up slopes, we learned how to cross-country ski along the way. Dad had taught himself when he and Mom had come to Yellowstone without Matt and me the previous winter. Matt, like Dad, picked up the rhythms and techniques naturally. Neither Mom nor I were graced with the genetics for athleticism—or even balance—yet here we were with them. Or maybe they were there with us, hoisting us up when we pitched sideways on the flats or toppled backward on slight inclines.

"Be careful," a man on the shuttle told us when he heard our destination. "Someone died on that trail earlier this season."

I could see how. When we finally got across the flats, the trail slipped into a slim opening between the trees, revealing a series of steep switchbacks. Matt, true to his *How hard can it be?* approach to life, disappeared from view, confident he could learn on the way down. Dad coached Mom and me about how to descend the precipitous drop. I didn't want to do it, but this was the only way back. Even if we decided we could go no farther and returned to the trailhead, the shuttle wasn't coming through again until the next day. So I made my way down, one cautious, clumsy, gravity-fighting move at a time. My skis took turns I didn't mean to take and moved faster than I wanted to go, and I worried I would become the season's second fatality on that trail.

Like Matt, Dad took the descent with relative ease. Mom, who insisted the rest of us go first, left the safety of the top only because the thought of the family stranded overnight in the wilderness was worse than attempting the slope. Like me, she fell. On every switchback. And on every one, Dad hauled himself back up the trail to rescue her.

Our server was right. We had been out skiing. We'd faced the wilderness and made it back alive. I hurt everywhere but, uncharacteristically, I didn't mind. Something in me had shifted.

"Maybe you should apply for a job out here this summer," Dad said after our server stepped away. "You like Yellowstone. You're good with people. You know enough about the park to be helpful. I think you'd enjoy it."

I scanned the dining room. The waitstaff was busy, but they weren't simply shuttling food from kitchen to table. Most were standing, relaxed and smiling, deep in conversation with their customers. I pictured myself in the scene, clad in the requisite beige skirt, shirt, and vest with a maroon paisley ascot around my neck. Neither uniforms nor waiting tables had ever interested me, but Dad was right.

I liked Yellowstone. I liked helping people. I probably would enjoy it.

A few days later, we headed home—alive and intact—with an application for summer employment in my backpack. By March I'd been offered a contract to work in the housekeeping department at Lake Lodge. Both the position and the location were second choices—housekeeping because I wanted to be with park visitors, not alone in their empty rooms, and Lake because it wasn't Old Faithful. Second choices or not, the job was in Yellowstone, so I signed.

We returned at the end of May, arriving at the East Entrance two days after my high school graduation. We paid our twenty-dollar fee for the week and entered the park. From there, we took the steadily climbing road to Sylvan Pass, more than fifteen hundred feet above. Faced with the unnerving experience of hurtling over a mountain highway perched on pylons, Mom clutched the door handle as tightly as the pavement clung to the mountainside. Eventually, the curves, drop-offs, and sweeping panoramas got to her, reviving her dormant motion sickness at the same moment Dad pointed out a large, dark mammal outlined against the vibrant spring verdure.

"Look! It's a moose," he exclaimed.

Such sightings were rare for our family, as are exclamations from my dad. Still, he pulled over and waited. After Mom regained her composure he said, "I hate to be indelicate, but would you mind going back to look at that moose?"

Dad drove to a turnout and stopped. There, now partially hidden among the vegetation, stood a moose placidly going about the business of filling its stomach. Tall, dark, and gangly in comparison to the small, delicate, deer-like creature I expect to see, moose are magnificent. Still, something about them is inexplicably impossible-looking, as though they'd been fashioned from spare bits and pieces.[1]

Mom wasn't the only one with a queasy stomach. Mine, though, had nothing to do with the road. Yellowstone was a thousand miles from home. I wasn't sure I was ready.

Four hours, eighty-five miles, and a handful of stops later, we pulled up in front of the employment center for my one o'clock appointment. I got out of our maroon station wagon, waved to Mom, Dad, and Matt, crossed the parking lot, and entered a building as drab as the dining room staff's uniforms. Inside, I presented my contract to the woman behind the counter. She looked at it and frowned, then opened a heavy black binder, its pages dog-eared and ragged and its cover cracked and flaking.

"That's what I thought," she muttered to herself. Then, to me, "Lake Lodge housekeeping is full. We overhire because we get a lot of no-shows."

With that, she turned toward a woman standing among the rows of file cabinets deep in the room. "This girl is here to work housekeeping at Lake Lodge and it's full."

Watching them confer, I worried about what that meant for me. We'd driven an awfully long way to discover I didn't have a job because of a hiring miscalculation. The woman returned to the counter and rifled through the binder again. "We can reassign you—if you'd be willing to work as a gift shop cashier at the Old Faithful Inn. The pay is $3.50, ten cents an hour less than housekeeping."

I wasn't there for the money. I was there to experience the things that made Yellowstone, Yellowstone. After the deductions for room and board, my check wouldn't amount to much anyway. I'd wanted to work in the gift shop at the Old Faithful Inn, but I'd been happy enough to settle for housekeeping at Lake Lodge, a

---

1. Placid and impossible-looking or not, moose are not only fast runners and proficient swimmers, they can be territorial and are solid enough to derail a train. As with all of Yellowstone's animals, they're wild. It's not only best for them to be observed from a distance, it's best for us too.

place I'd never even seen. Interaction with park visitors and living in the Old Faithful area was worth far more than the four extra dollars a week I would earn cleaning empty rooms at a different location. This wasn't a miscalculation. It was a gift—maybe even a miracle.

Elated, I signed a new contract and floated back to my waiting family, two beige uniforms clutched to my chest.

2 THE ENTOURAGE

More than four million people visit Yellowstone each year, and the majority of them make the pilgrimage to Old Faithful. Part of the Upper Geyser Basin, it's surrounded not only by forest but also by three hotels, seven restaurants, two gas stations, a Visitor Education Center, a ranger station, two grocery stores, a medical clinic, and an official post office. A small city tucked away in the woods, the Old Faithful area swarms with people and their vehicles. The Old Faithful Inn presides over it all, flags flying from the four corners of its roof by day and golden light from its antiquated lamps flickering through its dormer windows by night.

When my family made our first visit to Yellowstone in 1981, we arrived at the Old Faithful area shortly after sunset, welcomed to the Inn by the warm glow it cast into the falling darkness. Those were the days before the Internet and the proliferation of books devoted to the lodges of the National Park System. None of us had even seen a picture of the Inn. Dad had heard about it from a coworker and booked a room.

"We get to stay here?" Mom asked, awed by the enchanting log castle in the wilderness.

Six years later, I got to live there. It was where I worked, where

I ate, and where I stopped on my way from one place to another. While I slept in a dorm surrounded by pines a half mile away, the Inn was the center of my waking hours. Situated just a few feet from Old Faithful's boardwalk, it was more than a place bustling with people busy about the business of leisure and commerce. It was more than a shelter for the weary, the adventurous, and the bored.

It was home.

Even though it was Dad who suggested I apply for a summer job in Yellowstone, it wasn't easy for him to leave me there. He, Mom, and Matt spent a week in the park, hiking and visiting our favorite places while I attended orientation and training, both of which took place at Mammoth Hot Springs. When I finished, they drove me down to Old Faithful, moved me into my room, and stayed one final night. The next morning, before my first official shift, we said goodbye outside of my dorm. Watching them drive away, I felt as alone in the middle of the bustling Old Faithful area as I had when the ski shuttle had dropped the four of us off in the wilderness the previous winter. Only this time, I really was alone.

Because most visitors to the Old Faithful area come only for an eruption and leave as soon as it's finished, predicted eruption times are posted throughout the area. As a volunteer at the visitor center, I predicted Old Faithful's eruptions using a stopwatch and a tree.[1] With a sketch of the tree as a graph by which to measure the high point of the water, I plotted the intersection between the length and height of the current eruption. This equated to the

---

1. While my actual job was at the gift shop, I volunteered for a shift each week at the visitor center. I didn't know anyone else who did this but, it was like my dad said. I liked Yellowstone. I was good with people. And I knew enough about the park to be helpful.

predicted time for the next one. No matter who made the prediction, it always carried this disclaimer: plus or minus ten minutes.

Those minutes dictated the rhythm of the gift shop. When visitors arrived only to discover they had "missed it" ("it" being an eruption), they descended on our store. Busloads and carloads of people crammed inside. They coiled around displays and each other—some on the hunt, others killing time—until the clock silently compelled them to form a line that snaked deep into the recesses of the shop. The customers at the front were friendly and talkative; they had plenty of time to make their purchases and get to the boardwalk. Those farther back shot accusing looks at cashiers who by habit, by nature, and by necessity chatted with their customers about Yellowstone—listening to stories, answering questions, and offering tips. The shoppers at the end of the line grumbled that Old Faithful was "scheduled to go off" in eight (or six, or four, or maybe even two) minutes, not understanding—or maybe not accepting—that geysers keep their own rhythm and there was no scheduling about it. Then, either by success or surrender, they were gone. With the shop empty and quiet, we restored order by restocking the pillaged postcard wall and refolding mountains of ransacked T-shirts.

When I arrived one morning for the midday shift, a girl from my dorm met me at the gift shop's double door. "Did you hear?" she gushed. "The crown prince of Iran and his entourage are here at Old Faithful today."

I hadn't heard. I'd never seen an entourage and wondered if I'd know one if I saw it. Envisioning an energetic group in exotic attire, I slipped behind the camera counter, my assigned station for the day.

It was 1987, long before digital cameras and smartphones. Visitors who wanted to take nothing but pictures needed a steady stream of supplies—supplies we sold. We stocked film for 110 cartridge and 35mm cameras, as well as Polaroid instants, along with batteries to keep them going. We also carried a couple of cameras, although I'd never seen them removed from the glass case. So, when one of the assistant managers came to the counter and said, "Natalie, these guests would like to purchase a camera," I moved aside to make room for him. But he didn't step behind the counter. He simply smiled and walked away, leaving me alone with the cluster of solemn twenty-somethings curved shoulder to shoulder in two tight lines around the display case.

They didn't make a sound. Their clothes were far from exotic. But I knew. This was the entourage.

Taking a deep breath, I unlocked the sliding door, pulled out the two cameras, and set them on the glass countertop. "These are the cameras we carry. They're both point-and-shoot Kodaks."

Nearly a dozen sets of dark, unblinking eyes looked back at me expectantly. Those two sentences contained everything I knew about those cameras. Regretting my inattention during journalism class, I reached under the display case to unearth the camera boxes and set them on the counter where I could see the differentiating details. The whole group listened in silence while I went over the selling points of each one, my shaking hands concealed behind my back. When, by turn, they began asking questions, I realized that they hadn't just popped in to pick up a camera. They had stopped to shop for one, and I was going to have to sell it.

To all of them.

I had figured if I ever had to sell a camera, it would be to a little family from, say, Kansas, not a foreign entourage complete with armed guards. The little family from Kansas would have come to the counter, told me they wanted to buy a camera, and then spent more time talking about their adventures in the park than considering their purchase. Then they would have handed over their traveler's checks or their credit card and dashed out the door. It would be easy, like selling a T-shirt.

But this wasn't a little family from Kansas. And it wasn't easy.

Feeling ill-equipped to speak intelligently about photography and unnerved by the prospect of attempting it in front of the crown prince of anywhere, I looked out over the entourage and surveyed the store for backup—the kind we often gave each other in the form of presence or help, standing beside a coworker who was on the receiving end of a tirade or bagging items to speed up a sluggish line. The store was quiet, and all my coworkers stood motionless—mannequins at their empty stations. It was obvious. No one, not my manager and not my coworker who'd met me so enthusiastically at the door that morning, was going to back me up. I was on my own. Then Donna, a sweet little gray-haired lady from Nebraska, met my gaze and smiled at me from her place behind the jewelry counter.

It was enough.

I took another deep breath and found the words I needed to explain what they wanted to know. And they wanted to know a lot. For a very long time. While they all asked questions, one man—probably the crown prince—decided which camera to buy. I rang it up, along with enough batteries and film to last them a while. They paid in cash and left at the same unhurried pace they displayed during the sale and purchase of the camera.

Donna was at my side before the last of the entourage had passed through the double door. "Well done, Natalie. That was hard, and you handled it well."

I smiled. Handling a royal entourage from any country was a lot for a fresh-out-of-high-school, small-town girl. That Donna had paid attention—that she had smiled when I needed to see it and encouraged me when I needed to hear it—mattered. I hadn't been alone, even when I had felt like it.

3 WAKING UP IN YELLOWSTONE

"I could never work at Old Faithful," the guy across the counter groused, handing me his employee I.D. "If I worked here, I'd have to live here. I'm at Lake, where it's quiet. How can you stand it with all these people? It's so crowded."

I'd heard this before, from other employees visiting from other parts of the park. Old Faithful was too crowded. Too developed. Too touristy. I didn't disagree. It was all of those things.

But I loved it—as did everyone I knew who lived and worked there. Loving a place is much like loving a person: complicated. None of us loved the crowds, but we loved the Inn's architecture and its ambiance, as well as our daily commute along Old Faithful's boardwalk. And I loved the rhythms of the gift shop—including the sea of humanity that surged in and out in sync with the gravitational pull of the geyser. Living and working near Old Faithful was worth it. Loving the Inn meant appreciating it for what it was not as much as for what it was.

Besides, "all these people" made my work interesting. Sometimes they ranted about creaking radiators, crawling traffic, or the chaotic state of the forest floor. Sometimes they wanted to tell someone what they'd seen. Sometimes they asked questions. Where can we see a bear? When do the elk turn into moose? Where do the rangers keep the animals at night?

Standing across the camera counter from the man who asked that last one, I almost laughed. Surely he was joking. But I looked at him and saw he was serious. *This guy has to be at least thirty.* I thought. *How could he not know this?* There is no way to contain Yellowstone's animals. Even if there was, that's not what the park is about. I envisioned rangers summoning animals of all kinds—big ones like bison, bears, moose, and elk, along with small ones like foxes, marmots, otters, and mice—toward iron bars rising from the earth to contain them for the night. Setting the image aside, I smiled and answered him. "The animals stay out all day and all night. Some wear collars for observation, but rangers don't interfere much with the natural way of things."

His eyes widened. "Oh. Wow."

It didn't matter how he didn't know. What mattered was that he wanted to. That kind of curiosity and learning is what Yellowstone is about. He'd asked the question, but it was a good lesson for me.

While Yellowstone's woods, wildlife, and waterfalls are worthwhile on their own, it's the geysers that set it apart from other parks. A geyser, according to the National Park Service, is "a hot spring that erupts periodically." While scientifically accurate, it's a lifeless depiction of a life-altering phenomenon. Like comprehending the immensity of the ocean or Niagara Falls, absorbing the magnitude of a geyser is most easily done in person. They occur in only a handful of places around the globe. More than half the world's total are in Yellowstone. Among them, Old Faithful is the most famous, probably due to tall tales about its dependability. Lore aside, its eruptions don't occur every hour on the hour. It has a rhythm of its own, one with patterns we can see and eruptions we can accurately predict. Just as it did during the

1870s when the Washburn Expedition explored the Upper Geyser Basin, it erupts today with the regularity that earned it its name.[1]

Much of the time, a thin column of steam rises from Old Faithful, a silent hint of what's going on beneath the surface. While each one is different, an imminent eruption is generally indicated by thick, rolling steam and a short spurt. After some intermittent splashing and a big slosh or two, water shoots straight from its cone, higher and higher in a steady stream. Billowing steam rises into the air above, mingling with the clouds or, on a clear day, simply drifting off. Gradually, the height of the column of water drops until only steam remains. This is what we see above ground.

Below, heat from magma in the earth increases the temperature of water that has seeped underground until it passes the boiling point, superheating it until the pressure becomes so great that it's forced through whatever outlet it finds. This results in what we think of as an eruption. In Old Faithful's case, the outlet is a small vent in the earth's surface through which water and steam shoot almost two hundred feet into the air at regular intervals. That this happens at all is astounding. That it's ours to witness, understand, and even predict is miraculous.

Like the guy who "could never work" at Old Faithful, my coworkers and I hiked and explored other parts of the park

---

1. The 1870 Washburn-Langford-Doane Expedition, often referred to as the Washburn Expedition, officially explored the area that became Yellowstone in 1872. Washburn's contribution was commemorated via a mountain that bears his name: Mount Washburn. While a moderately strenuous, six-mile round-trip hike will take you to its summit, the parking lot from the Chittenden Road trailhead also offers a lovely prospect. Truman Everts, another member of the Washburn Expedition, became separated from the group early on and spent more than a month wandering alone in the wilderness before being rescued. He, too, has a mountain named after him: Mount Everts near Mammoth Hot Springs. His story is included in the Resources and Reading List at the end of this book.

together during our time off. One day, though, all my usual hiking companions were on duty.

I decided to hike to Mystic Falls. Alone.

From my dorm, I walked to the sprawling back parking lot and wound past the Snow Lodge, the visitor center, Old Faithful, and the Inn. Then, from the smaller front parking lot, I joined the long loop around the Upper Geyser Basin. Following it to Morning Glory Pool, I left the boardwalk and the comforting bustle of the crowd and stepped into the woods for my first solo hike. To bolster my confidence, I breathed deep, relishing the scents of sulfur and pine carried on the crisp morning air. Within a few steps, I arrived at the trailhead. Posted there was a temporary sign featuring the outline of a bear and these words:

WARNING
BEAR
FREQUENTING AREA

I paused to consider my options. Already nervous about my solitary trek into the wilderness, my anxiety soared. *What am I supposed to do? Turn back? Proceed with caution?* Yellowstone is not a zoo. Bears have free range. One could be in any place, at any time. At least that's what I'd been told. In all my time in the park, I'd never actually seen one, but I took it on faith they were there. Apparently, someone had seen one in this area, but how long ago? Did it even matter?

Happy-looking hikers approached the trailhead from the direction of the falls—notably unhurried and uneaten. Other hikers stepped off the boardwalk behind me, glanced at the sign, and headed down the trail without so much as a hitch in their pace. That, it seemed, was how it was done. Taking another deep breath, I stepped past the sign and into the wild.

Geyserite crunched beneath my feet as I walked through sparse forest toward the Grand Loop road, where I emerged into civilization long enough to cross the pavement to Biscuit Basin's boardwalk.² Entering a thicker wood, the trail followed a small, bubbling stream. Mostly what you see on a hike through the forest is trees. In the case of an old growth lodgepole pine forest, what you see are tree trunks because shade from the top branches causes the lower ones to wither. Tall, dense, and close, trees and trunks alike surround you with dappled light and fairy-tale solitude. It's wonderful—magical even—if you are with other people. But I wasn't with other people. And anyone who's ever read the grim version of a Grimm's fairy tale knows forests are dangerous places with dark, ominous underpinnings. Their enveloping shelter prevents you from seeing anything until it—whatever *it* might be—is right in front of you. Or, in the case of a bear, you are right in front of it.

I tried to be brave, or at least look it, but with each scan of the terrain ahead, every peripheral peek or backward glance, I felt like a meerkat from *The Lion King* forced out into the open. All the way to Mystic Falls, every time a fellow hiker came into view I was torn between relief that someone else had taken this trail and lived and the temptation to turn and tail them back to the safety of the boardwalk.

When I finally reached Mystic Falls, I forced myself to walk to the water's edge at the base. By nature, I'm a waterfall person. Under normal conditions, I would have lingered—lounging on a rock like a cat in the sun, listening to the melody of the water dancing down the rugged falls. But these were not normal conditions. I was alone. In the wilderness. On a trail frequented—at some point in recent history—by a bear. After reaching the river, I

---

2. As close to the main road as Biscuit Basin is, even there the "wild" in Yellowstone's wilderness has exerted itself. During the summer of 2024, an explosion occurred in the middle of the day near a busy boardwalk in Biscuit Geyser Basin, ejecting steam and debris and destroying a section of the wooden walkway. Apparently, such explosions happen regularly--but usually not in areas of the park frequented by a lot of people. With its roads, parking lots, and places of commerce, it's easy to forget that Yellowstone is a wild place.

turned and—without lingering for even a moment—meerkatted my way back to civilization.

When the trailhead came into view, I resisted the urge to hug the sign and instead took solace in the swarm of people on the boardwalk. Taking my place among the masses making their way through the Upper Geyser Basin, I looked up at the lodgepole-covered mountains visible above the thermal haze. I'd hiked into the wilderness alone. Just as I'd done with my family the previous winter, I'd faced the lonely trail and survived.

My next stop was the post office, a place I could reach via a detour past Old Faithful. When I arrived, I took a seat, not needing to check the next predicted eruption time. Every bench sat empty while the famous geyser's public was off shopping or eating or walking the boardwalk. I would be waiting a while. And that was okay.

I lived in the middle of a miracle. Every morning, I woke up in Yellowstone. I walked the path between the trees, each new day's unbroken silence carried on air soaked with sulfur and pine. I watched Old Faithful erupt whenever I wanted—as long as I was willing to wait. It wasn't perfect and it wasn't always easy, but living in the wilderness was teaching me to follow its rhythms. Rhythms that revealed a universe that runs by a clock I can't set. Rhythms that gave gifts disguised as miscalculations. Rhythms that invited me to linger over the landscape and protected me from living a lukewarm life.

That something that had started to shift on the previous winter's cross-country ski trail was my soul. It was waking up.

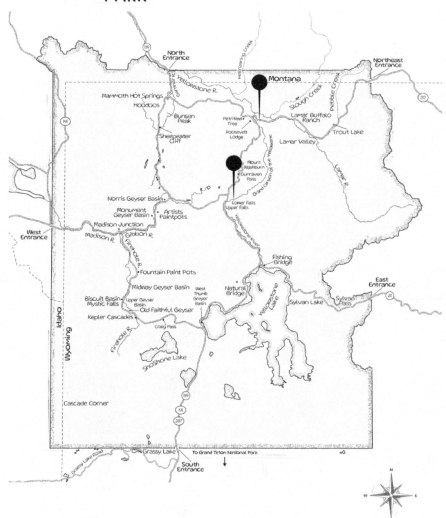

4 BEAR COUNTRY

In 1981, when Matt was eight and I was twelve, Mom and Dad took us to Yellowstone for the first time. After packing our Buick Skylark with suitcases and picnic supplies, they drove us a thousand miles across Iowa, Nebraska, South Dakota, and Wyoming. It was a decision and an act of generosity I grossly underappreciated.

They wanted to show us there was more to life than malls and movies. What was really on our minds, though—on *all* our minds—were bears. Even Matt, who earned the nickname Eagle Eyes by spotting wildlife of all kinds and sizes, didn't see one. Still, we looked for them everywhere. While we couldn't find one anywhere, we believed in their presence around every corner, behind every boulder, and in every patch of dry grass—a belief fueled by official park service signs that read:

BEAR COUNTRY
Store all food in vehicle
Read bulletin board regulations
All wildlife are dangerous.

These words also bound us to places of perceived safety: busy paved roads and heavily peopled boardwalks. Yellowstone's several hundred miles of road kept us occupied from Dad's predawn wake-up call until September's early darkness. During the days of train travel, this road was shaped by stagecoaches transporting visitors through the park. It paralleled Yellowstone Lake's shoreline, traveled through tunnels of towering trees, offered access to several scenic drives, and provided easy passage to every major geyser basin. More than fifteen miles of boardwalk wound through Yellowstone's most popular destinations—including the thermal areas. Much to Matt's chagrin and mine, Mom and Dad insisted we visit them all. While I was awed by Yellowstone's wildlife and otherworldly landscape, I was a kid with a kid's aversion to visitor centers and an affinity for sleeping in the car.

"Wake up," Dad would say when he discovered Matt or I had drifted off. "You can sleep at home." He didn't want us to miss a thing.

The Grand Canyon of the Yellowstone was no exception. Grousing as loudly as I dared, I got out of the station wagon in yet another parking lot and trudged along behind my family to see yet another sight. Hidden behind some scrubby trees, a short stone staircase led to an up-close view of both the canyon and the Upper Falls. There, we not only saw the Yellowstone River lose its footing, we felt its power when it found it again after a free fall of more than one hundred feet. It was enough to create a crack in my teenage indifference. *All this is here? We could have driven past and never known.*

It wasn't long before we stopped again to make our way through another parking lot and down another asphalt sidewalk. But this time, Dad left the crowd and led us toward a path between the pines. Our destination this time was the brink of the Lower Falls which, at over three hundred feet, is Yellowstone's tallest waterfall. Over switchbacks swagged like ribbon across the canyon wall, the trail gave up six hundred feet of elevation in just three-tenths of a mile. Translation: it was steep.

After our descent into the canyon, I not only heard the

pounding of all those thousands of gallons of water pouring over the riverbed's rock ledge, I also felt, for the very first time, the weight of the wilderness.

I didn't like it. That kind of power had its place and I had mine—far from the stone barrier between me and the brink of the falls with its backdrop of mist rising from the frothing river. Unperturbed by the intensity, my parents and brother lingered at the barricade while I lurked near the trail. When they finally turned to go, my happiness was short-lived. The way out was as steep as the way in, only this time we were walking up.

With Matt by my side and Mom and Dad right behind us, I trudged along, head down and eyes fixed on the ground three feet in front of me, my view limited to the moss thriving in the humid air at the base of a multitude of towering lodgepole pines. As we approached the hairpin turn that would take the trail in the opposite direction, the four of us gasped in unison and, as a single unit, froze. Not two feet off the trail ahead of us was a bear—sprawled on the black dirt, the snout on its big brown head pointed at our shoes. Nothing moved. Not our lungs. Not our feet. Not the bear. That's when we—again, as a unit—realized our imaginations had tricked us. It wasn't a bear. It was a log—damp, dark, and decaying in the same misty air that nurtured the moss—its center section jutting out and looking, to our green, jittery eyes, like the nose on a bear's face.

It would be typical—expected even—for me to see a bear where none existed, but not for the rest of the family. Not for my eagle-eyed brother. Not for my sensible mother or my logical father. But Yellowstone isn't typical. It's bear country, a place that can wreak havoc on the mind. As for us, we were just happy to be wrong. Glad to be alive. Grateful, for once, to not see a bear.

Two Septembers later we were back. Mom and Dad had visited Yellowstone without Matt and me during the year in between.

They'd ventured away from the security of the road and the boardwalks and returned unharmed and uneaten. Now they were ready to get the whole family onto the trail.

I was not a happy hiker. But because Mom and Dad weren't about to leave me alone in a parking lot while they took Matt and traipsed off into the woods, I followed along, sometimes pouting, other times allowing the warmth of the afternoon sun to brighten my mood. The rest of the family didn't need their moods brightened. Dad loved hiking. Mom pushed herself to do whatever the family did. Matt was a ten-year-old boy, stronger and more adventurous than I was.

Trails, typically designated easy, moderate, or strenuous, sometimes are distinct dirt paths. Sometimes they diverge, without a clear indication of which one to follow. And sometimes they lead to an open meadow where hikers find themselves searching for blazes—orange metal flags fastened to tree trunks to mark the way.

Inexperienced as we were, the trail to the petrified forest on Specimen Ridge was a problem from the beginning.[1] We walked up seemingly endless grassy slopes in search of blazes. Small to begin with, they fade with time and exposure—not exactly the makings of unfailing beacons of light. After a while, it became obvious we should have found the forest of petrified trees by now and agreed together it would be a good idea for Dad and Matt—because they're fast—to go ahead and hike over the next hill. If they found the fossilized forest, they'd come back for Mom and me. If not, we would head back to the car.

It made sense.

At least, it made sense until Dad and Matt disappeared over the crest of the hill, and Mom and I realized that we were alone in exactly the kind of meadow we'd been telling each other a bear

---

1. I've shared a few stories from this book on the internet—primarily on my website, natalieogbourne.com, and at anthemoftheadventurer.com. This would be one of those stories.

would spend a sunny afternoon in. We wanted to see a bear but not on the trail. And most definitely not on the trail without Dad and Matt.

"What if a bear comes?" I asked Mom.

Mom, always practical and always applying her nurse's tendency to follow procedure, asked, "Well, what did the hiking book say to do?"

"I read something about climbing a tree. And I've heard something about dropping your backpack to distract the bear too. If it charges, you're supposed to get down on the ground, curl up in the fetal position, and play dead."

The fetal position we could pull off, but we were utterly backpackless. Looking around, I saw nothing we could climb—no short, branching fruit trees or sprawling oaks. Yellowstone is largely forested by lodgepole pines—sun-loving trees that shoot for the sky, their trunks so long and straight they were named for their use in the construction of lodges built by some American Indian tribes. Their upper branches shade the ones below, causing the understory to shrivel and die from lack of sun. The few pines in the previously friendly-looking meadow held their branches high in the sky like a grove of Christmas trees perched atop telephone poles and looked to be climbable only by an animal equipped with claws. An animal like a cat. Or a bear.

Mom and I looked at each other and laughed.

"Maybe," said Mom, sobering, "we should give it a try. Just in case."

We made our way to the closest tree, stood at the base, and looked up. It might as well have been Everest. "If this is what they say to do, maybe it isn't that hard," she encouraged.

Undeterred by the absence of branches within grabbing distance, she walked to the most suitable-looking specimen and wove her fingers into a stirrup for me to step into. This, had it been successful, would have added two, maybe three feet to my five foot three inches, woefully short of the fifteen needed to grasp the lowest branch. We laughed and collapsed in a heap.

It was obvious. If a bear came over the mountain before Dad and Matt returned, we were going to die.

Apparently, climbing a tree *is* that hard. At least it's that hard with no actual bear to spur you on or if you aren't a climber by nature. And, much like dropping your backpack, it isn't recommended anymore, anyway—especially if the bear you're trying to avoid is *Ursus americanus*, the American black bear, with its long, curved, tree-climbing claws. It makes sense. Training bears to forage for food from hikers' backpacks and fighting one in a tree are both bad ideas.

That was in 1983. According to a conversation with a park ranger, the grizzly bear population that year was around 200. Even with all our looking and wondering, we didn't see one. They were out there, though. I knew it.

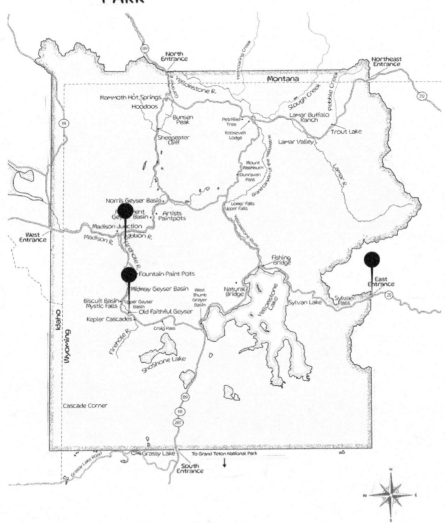

5 THIS WAY, BABE

Jaime, my husband of two years, sprinted up the steps to our apartment and dropped his messenger bag beside the door. "Ready to go?"

He'd just finished the last final of his junior year at Iowa State University. If he'd slept the night before, it had been a catnap at his desk. Still, this was his first trip to Yellowstone, and he was as ready to go as our packed and waiting car. Within minutes, he'd settled into the driver's seat, where he stayed until we reached our night's hotel in northwest Nebraska.

The next morning, I walked out of our room and down the hall until I heard his voice, "This way, Babe." I looked around, certain the stairs were up ahead, only to discover I was headed toward a dead end. I turned around and, together, we descended the open staircase, crossed the lobby to the glass double doors, and left the building. A few steps into the parking lot I heard him again. "This way, Babe." Without bothering to look around, I pivoted and followed his voice to where he stood, waiting. He held out his hand. Jaime instinctively always knows where he is and I, just as instinctively, do not.

Jaime drove north to Mount Rushmore and west toward Yellowstone, until road trip-induced adrenaline gave way to finals week sleep deprivation, and he announced he was too tired to keep driving. Four years older than Jaime, I was past the trials of end-of-semester tests. It was my turn, a word that implies I carry my weight as a driver. I don't. I usually drive all of an anemic hour, long enough for him to catch a catnap but not an actual break. That day, though, I kept driving, and Jaime kept sleeping. While I drove, I calculated our progress.

We were making good time.

The roads that lead to Yellowstone make it clear. You can get there from here. All you have to do is follow the signs. Whether I followed one claiming to be the most scenic route, the shortest route, or even the fastest, I was in familiar territory. I could choose my own adventure.

Over an early dinner at an A&W in Sheridan, Wyoming, I said, "I've been thinking."

"What about?" asked Jaime, immediately on guard. Those three words preceded every HGTV DIY project I imagined would be easy for me but inevitably created a lot of work for him.

"We're making good time," I said. "Really good time. Actually, we're a few hours ahead of schedule. We could make it to Yellowstone tonight instead of tomorrow morning. We're only a couple hundred miles from the park. I think we could get to the Inn by ten. We'd just need to call and find out if there's a room available."

He looked relieved. "Sounds good," he said, and we left in search of a pay phone.

Returning to the car after procuring a reservation, he asked if I was tired and offered to drive.

"No, I'm fine," I answered. "I can keep going."

Jaime looked surprised. I'd never passed up an opportunity to escape the driver's seat. "Are you sure?"

"Yeah. I'm doing just fine. Thanks, though."

"Okay," he said after a short pause, then started up the John Grisham audiobook we'd brought along to entertain ourselves on the nearly twenty-four-hour road trip.

We headed out of town straight into a heavy spring sleet. Our puny red Plymouth Sundance plodded down the highway along with semis that seemed determined to bury us under a layer of blinding slush. A quick stop for gas revealed that we were woefully unprepared for the western weather. It was nothing short of wintery.

We could have been prepared. While we were packing, Jaime had asked if we would need winter coats. *Winter coats? Why would we need winter coats? It's May. We'll be in Yellowstone. It will be perfect.* That's what I said in my head. Out loud it was something more along the lines of, "No. I don't think so."

Jaime looked doubtful but shrugged and said, "Okay. You're the one who lived there. You would know," and returned to his packing. And now he knew the truth: when it came to Yellowstone's weather, I could not be trusted.

At 8:45 that night we found a Kmart on the outskirts of Cody, Wyoming. We dashed through the arctic air to the entrance where, right inside the front door, a clearance rack hawked the paltry remains of its winter stock. One dollar and fifty cents later we emerged, saved by two sets of gloves and two hats.

"I can drive," offered Jaime as we approached the car.

I was already headed for the driver's side, keys clutched in my hand. "No thanks. I can keep going," I told him. As I exited the parking lot, I noticed he was staring at me. "What are you looking at?" I asked.

"Just trying to figure out what's gotten into you. You've been driving all day. You haven't gotten tired. You haven't panicked because of the traffic. You haven't gotten lost. It's just ... " He trailed off, mystified.

Under normal conditions, Cody is an hour's drive from Yellowstone's East Entrance. The sleet had finally stopped and I hoped we would make better time, but now the highway was serving as a crosswalk for every mule deer in Park County. It was the final obstacle between them and the Shoshone River where they seemed to be gathering for a nightcap. They traveled in small bands, and in nearly every one a single deer stood sentry on the shoulder while the others emerged from the woods and stepped with caution into the open and onto the roadway. They didn't dart. They didn't freeze in the headlights. They didn't vacillate over which way to go as our car bore down on them. Unlike the white-tail deer that litter the Iowa roadsides every autumn, they simply—without drama—crossed from one side to the other. Regardless of their traffic skills, all those deer made for a slow drive.

By ten o'clock, the hour of my overly optimistic ETA, we hadn't even made it to Yellowstone's border. When we finally reached the East Entrance, Old Faithful was still an hour and a half deeper into the park. Regardless, we were euphoric. We'd arrived! Our elation was short-lived, subdued almost immediately by a sign:

ROAD
CONSTRUCTION
AHEAD

Not far beyond, we encountered a second, equally dispiriting sign:

SPEED
LIMIT
25

That, combined with the discovery that the road had been reduced to its dirt base, was going to slow us down more than the deer had. Observing the speed limit had as much to do with concern for the structural integrity of our car as with obeying the law.

At the end of twenty painful miles, we had slogged over Sylvan Pass, driven the shoreline of the still-frozen Yellowstone

Lake, and arrived at a T-intersection that delivered us to intact pavement. There, a new sign informed us the short route to Old Faithful was closed. Snow removal, a process that begins in early March, was not yet complete. Even after two months of plowing, an unfinished Craig Pass stood between us and the fast route to our hotel. Like donkeys following a carrot, we kept driving and driving but our destination kept eluding us. Casting a longing look to the left, I turned right and continued our ever-lengthening journey.

Shining through a cloudless sky, the full moon revealed more signs, directing visitors to points of interest such as the Grand Canyon of the Yellowstone River, Norris Geyser Basin, and Madison Junction. While the latter is technically an intersection of roads, it is also where the Firehole and Gibbon Rivers converge, creating the Madison, a famed trout-fishing river that—together with the Jefferson and Gallatin Rivers—eventually becomes the Missouri. The moon reflected off the snow and illuminated the trees, the water, and the eerie towers of billowing steam that hovered above the geyser basins along the Firehole. Unable to overcome his finals week fatigue, Jaime slept through it all.

Whenever I stopped at an intersection, he stirred and asked if I needed help figuring out which way to go. I didn't. I knew exactly where we were, where we were going, and how to get there.

I just wanted to get there faster.

Good time had abandoned us long ago. Weary and longing to be out of the car and tucked into bed, we still had miles to travel, over roads unmercifully heaved by winter's frost. Potholes, one of which could have swallowed our car whole, made it impossible to achieve even the park's standard speed limit of forty-five miles per hour.

As I rounded a curve, a small band of bison mingling in the thermal haze appeared in the glow of our headlights. The same steam that surrounded the bison glazed the road. We slid right into their gathering—toward one in particular, a yearling whose terrified eyes locked with mine before she scrambled out of the way. Either my gasp or the grinding tires woke Jaime.

"What's up?" he asked.

I said nothing. The sliding car and the bison, their eyes following us as we drifted past, answered better than I could. Besides, I was too busy listening to the echo of my own lofty voice from the summer I'd worked at the Inn. When a coworker had told me a park visitor had hit a bison with a vehicle and killed it, I'd said, incredulous, "How do you hit a bison? It's not like they dart onto the road." Now I knew. After we emerged, unscathed, I drove on, chagrined and grateful that both the bison and our car had survived.

The potential for destruction and death deterred Jaime from falling asleep for a few miles. He watched for wildlife on the road and enjoyed the moonlit scenery beyond. Eventually, though, he succumbed to sleep and didn't stir again until I squeezed his hand.

"Hey Babe," I whispered. "We're here."

It was two in the morning, four hours past my calculated arrival time. Jaime got out of the car and stood still, absorbing the log structure in the light of the full moon. Satisfied by his appreciative "wow," I said, "Ready to go?" Hand in hand, we climbed the stairs from the parking lot, walked under the wooden awning, and stepped through the Old Faithful Inn's double red door.

When the iron latch on the immense wooden door dropped into place, the pressure of the drive dissolved in the solace of the Inn's familiar presence. The thud of the door and clank of its heavy bar echoed across the vastness of the still, spacious lobby, stirring my soul. For a full summer I'd worked to the cadence of that door, and in the seven years since, Yellowstone had been working on me. Jaime walked to the center of the lobby, staring— as first-time visitors do—six stories straight up into the recesses of the nearly century-old log ceiling.

I looked up, too, but not for long. I didn't need to see it. I *felt* it. I was home.

Content, I crossed to the registration desk to check in to the room that would be our home for the next seven nights. Nothing had changed. The paperwork, the maroon and white key fobs, the map burned in leather by Jim—the Inn's artist-in-residence since before my family started visiting until after my final day on the job—were all exactly as I remembered. When I finished checking in, I returned to Jaime and held out my hand.

"This way, Babe," I said, and walked toward the open log staircase that led to our room.

6 WELCOME TO YELLOWSTONE

I'm an early riser, even after a 2:00 a.m. arrival. Jaime is not an early riser, especially after a 2:00 a.m. arrival. Resisting the urge to pounce on him like a kid on Christmas morning shouting, "Wake up! Wake up! Wake up! We're here! We're here! We're here!" I disentangled myself from his arms and slid into the previous day's clothes. With a surprising level of stealth, I slipped out of the room and down the hall to one of the Inn's many pay phones. As I had often done at the end of a shift in the gift shop, I plopped down on a cushioned chair and called Mom and Dad. While they were nearly as excited for us to be in the park as I was, our call didn't take long. Unfortunately, because I'd left the room without bothering to put on shoes, I couldn't walk the boardwalk. My books were still in the car, which would require keys, which were back in the room along with my shoes, so I couldn't read. No one else was stirring, so I couldn't even watch people.

With time to fill and nothing to do, I roamed the silent halls and empty lobby, waiting for a reasonable time to wake Jaime up.

Entering the room less stealthily than I had exited, I whispered, "Hey Babe." Jaime stirred but didn't respond. I pulled back the curtains to let in a little light.

"What time is it?" he asked.

"Seven. I woke up at six." *Which means*, I thought, *we've already wasted a whole hour.*

"Why would you get up early on vacation? Vacations are for sleeping in." Jaime threw his arm across his face and turned away from the window.

I didn't know vacations were for sleeping in. I thought they were for getting out. When I was young, it was Dad who woke too early and stole out of the room before sunrise to wait for the clock to register a reasonable hour to rouse the family. More courageous than I, and with the forethought to take his shoes, he busied himself by walking the Upper Geyser Basin, watching Old Faithful erupt by the dim light of the emerging dawn, or checking to make sure the car had plenty of oil. He always returned while it was still early.

"We're in Yellowstone," he'd tell us. "You can sleep at home." Apparently, his ways had worn off on me.

"Well, I did leave for an hour so you could sleep," I said.

Before long, Jaime opened his eyes and started surveying the details he'd missed in the night, pointing out the rough-hewn vertical plank walls and the ledge lining the perimeter of the room a few inches below the wood ceiling. "Well, I guess we could get going," he said, stretching before putting his feet on the worn wooden floor. He gathered his clothes for the day and headed down the hall to the shower. Our room was in Old House, the original log structure built back during the winter of 1903 and 1904. To enjoy its charms required enduring its quirks—including communal restrooms.

Showered and ready to go, we walked out of our third-floor room, down the hall, and onto the mezzanine where we stood at the lodgepole pine railing, its surface worn smooth by a century of hands. Below, the lobby already teemed with tourists, some milling about and others staring into the spacious stories above, as Jaime had the night before. In the filtered morning light, his gaze traveled up the imposing log wall, across the line of the ceiling, and down the commanding four-hearth stone chimney, pausing for a moment to examine the clock affixed to its front. With its thirteen-foot pendulum and yard-long hands, it dwarfs the brave employees who traverse the narrow platform to maintain it. Before long Jaime was looking up again, this time at a series of wooden staircases that led to lofty perches where the orchestra played and visitors gathered to listen during the early days.

He crossed to the staircase, and I knew he wanted to explore the catwalks and crow's nest. But the stairway was gated and locked, just as it had been since an earthquake rocked Yellowstone in 1959. The Inn had stood, but the structural soundness of the upper recesses had been compromised—limiting it to the bellmen who go out on the roof to raise and lower the flags of the United States, Wyoming, Montana, and Idaho every morning and evening. Reluctantly, Jaime turned away. Soon he was pointing out details his engineer's eye picked up that I'd never noticed—places where the original logs had been reinforced and how the lobby's heating unit had been painted to blend with the wood.

Once he was satisfied with his grasp of the Inn's essentials, we took the stairs down to the main lobby. We walked through the red door—now standing open and silent—and out into the park, where the scent of pine from the trees and sulfur from the geysers mingled in the crisp morning air. We followed the wide sidewalk to Old Faithful, but I knew from its deserted boardwalk it was a ways from erupting. Turning toward the car, Jaime saw by daylight what the illuminating moon had hinted at the night before—the Inn's presiding presence over the Upper Geyser basin.

Once again, I slipped behind the wheel so Jaime could see what we'd driven across the country to see. When we merged onto the main road we met the pillars of vapor we'd passed the night before and he saw, for the first time, the Firehole—a hallowed fly fishing river named for its warm, steamy ways. Winding through the Upper Geyser Basin and past Black Sand, Biscuit, and Midway basins, it collects the thermal runoff that keeps it temperate and open through the coldest of Yellowstone's bitter winters. Steam rose from its surface into the chilled mountain air, blending with the clouds smudged across a cheerless sky. Lodgepole pines reached from the mountaintops that circled the cozy valley where clusters of bison milled about between the road and the river, many with their heads to the ground, devouring the early season's offering of tender, nutritious grass. While winter's foliage had done little more than fill their stomachs, spring's would strengthen their sagging flesh. The calves of the year had begun to arrive, leggy dots of red fur stationed beside the brown shaggy bodies of their massive mothers.

"Tell me when you're ready to stop for lunch. We're having one of your favorites," I said after a morning of driving.

"Now would be good. I saw a picnic area a ways back that looked like it might have places along the water," Jaime answered. Our morning's exploration had kept us close to the Firehole, and while we stopped to walk the boardwalk at every geyser basin, it was always the water that drew his eye.

After we carted the picnic basket, cooler, and camp stove to a spot close to the riverbank, Jaime went to the water. I watched him wander upstream and back down as I smoothed the vintage floral cloth over the table and simmered beef au jus. Just as he returned, the sky delivered what it had been promising all morning and we ate our sandwiches side by side, facing the Firehole under a sprinkling of rain.

"Wanna drive?" I asked after we loaded everything into the trunk. I handed him the keys and settled into the passenger seat with a surprising sense of loss. By day's end, Yellowstone would be a map in Jaime's head, and my flash of navigational glory would be over.

We continued north, past the dissipating steam of the thermal areas, through close lodgepole forest that only occasionally gave way to open sky, and found ourselves looking at water once again.

But it wasn't the inviting, accessible Firehole. It was the Yellowstone, a gossamer ribbon running through the length of the twenty-mile Grand Canyon of the Yellowstone a thousand feet below. An impressionist chasm, steely water and cornflower sky contrasted with the warm colors washed across its creamy walls—yellow from iron and sulfur in the rock and orange from a reaction between thermal heat and iron compounds.

From the parking lot, we set off on a short hike. Red Rock Point's decaying asphalt trail took us into the canyon over a series of switchbacks through the varied greens of a mossy pine forest still glistening from the morning's rain. It wasn't long, less than a mile, but the final descent down stone steps delivered us to a wooden viewing deck at eye-level across the canyon from the 308-foot drop over the Lower Falls. Sitting among the vivid formations for which Red Rock Point received its name, we watched the ribbon of river dissolve into froth and felt its mist settle on our skin.

This was one of the few trails we were able to take. Because it was early in the season, many of our hiking plans were hampered by lingering snow and the presence of bears. Drifts turned us back from Monument Geyser Basin, a backcountry thermal area. Signs denied us entrance to many trails, an early-season practice meant to create space between park visitors and bears focused on finding sustenance following their long winter slumber. Even the path to LeHardy Rapids, a site just off the road, was roped and guarded by a sign:

AREA CLOSED FOR
BEAR MANAGEMENT

Our inability to get on the trail gave us time to explore every roadside feature, creating a mental map of the geyser basins, scenic drives, lakes, waterfalls, and every viewpoint of the Grand Canyon of the Yellowstone, along with our favorite vistas, picnic spots, and waterside turnouts. More a fan of Yellowstone than of hiking,

I was okay with this. The idea of running into a bear on the trail filled me with dread. Our week was full, and we'd hardly left sight of the road.

On the day we left, I cried when we walked through the red door for the final time.

"Don't worry," Jaime said. "I'll bring you back."

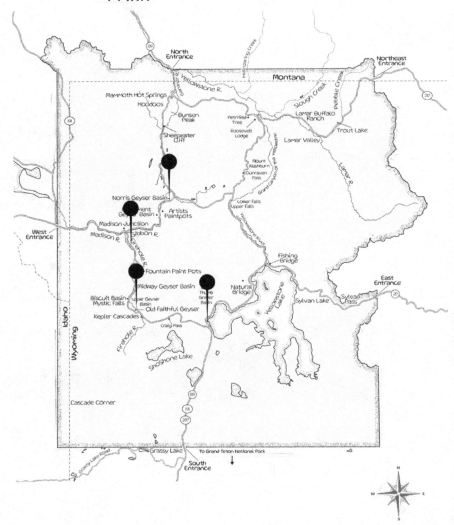

7 A LAND OF EXTREMES

Reducing his speed, our driver slowed, pulled to the edge of the groomed road, and turned to project his voice over the rumbling engine. "If you look back, you can see what we drivers call Teton Alley."

All eight passengers pivoted, our gazes sweeping down the ribbon of road stretched taut through the lodgepole pine forest behind us. Beyond the alley and above the trees, the snow-capped spires of Grand Teton National Park rose in the distance. When we finished looking, our driver resumed traveling speed, all thirty miles per hour of it, until we came upon a solitary bison. It was a bull—identifiable not because he had horns, but because he, like other adult males of his kind, was alone. He plodded along the edge of the snow-packed road, and our driver slowed and navigated to the far side to pass him. Nose straight ahead, the bison trotted along as though he hadn't noticed our presence. His eyes, though, darted wildly between us, the ground, and the way forward.

He knew we were there.

I was glad we were tucked safely inside the shelter of a snow-coach, entering Yellowstone the only way possible during winter

—on a track-driven vehicle.[1] Some people arrived by snowmobile, but we were staying for a week and a snowmobile couldn't have managed our luggage.

Jaime had been true to his word, bringing me back to Yellowstone several Septembers in a row. When we added children to our family, we brought them along while they were still in their infancy—our son making his first visit to the park at four months and our daughter at fifteen. This winter trip we decided to take on our own, leaving the kids back home in the care of their grandparents.

We'd boarded the snowcoach at Flagg Ranch, a small settlement between the Tetons and Yellowstone, and set off into the park's interior during its cold and comparatively untraveled season. This particular snowcoach was no converted twelve-passenger van or SUV. This was an historic bombardier.[2] Flamboyant yellow on the outside, inside its spartan benches were suited more to practicality than comfort. Propelled by tracks and steered by long skis, it was serviceable for winter. And it was loud, so loud it discouraged conversation and required our driver-cum-guide to shout. Because he worked summers at Yellowstone Lake's marina and spent his winters ferrying travelers in and out of Yellowstone, he knew the park. Intermittently, he called out bits of information over the engine's reverberations, seeking eye contact by looking at us in his oversized rearview mirror and occasionally pulling over and swinging around in his seat if he had a lot to say.

"What are y'all planning to do while you're here?" he hollered back at us.

A little discussion revealed we were all planning to cross-

---
1. Aside from the highway between Gardiner and Silver Gate, Montana, Yellowstone's roads are not plowed during the late fall and winter months. Weather permitting, the remaining roads open to oversnow vehicles in mid to late December. Snow removal, which begins in late February or early March, continues into May.
2. Yellowstone's bombardiers were an invention of Joseph-Armand Bombardier. While he is widely known for aircraft, his early work focused on snow travel.

country ski or snowshoe backcountry trails and snowmobile park roads. That settled, we shouted back and forth for a while about the current controversy over the proposed winter use policy. A movement was afoot to quiet the park, to study the pressure that visitors' wintertime activities put on the resident wildlife, and possibly even cap the number of vehicles allowed to enter the park each day. Already, while any snowmobile could be driven into Yellowstone, those available for rent within the park had been switched from the traditional, noisy two-stroke engine to the quieter four-stroke models. Transporting park visitors into Yellowstone's winter quiet creates noise, destroying the silence people want to experience and disrupting the survival efforts of the wildlife they hope to see. The goal was to lessen the impact on the animals during the park's harsh winter months. The changes, both rumored and actual, gave snowmobiling the look of an endangered species.

"You know what they'll come after next, once they get the noise from the snowmobiles under control, don't you?" The driver paused. "They're going to come after these."

He gave the dashboard an affectionate pat, like Mike Mulligan might have given to his beloved steam shovel. This was his vehicle. He took pride in driving it, in transporting park visitors, and in teaching them about Yellowstone along the way. He'd been driving that same machine, dubbed the *Millennium Falcon*, for four winters.

He brightened, telling us he'd faced similar concerns before and had been pleasantly surprised at the outcome. Back when the original Old Faithful Snow Lodge, a cramped and dark little building with a very seventies vibe, was demolished and replaced by a big and bright yet cozy mountain lodge, he worried the winter clientele would change. He thought maybe the people who came to the park because they thrived in the outdoors, because they loved Yellowstone, because they wanted to finally make that trip they'd been dreaming about, would be replaced by people simply looking for a place to spend their money. That, in his opinion, had not happened.

Just beyond Grant Village, we turned east. "We're going to walk around West Thumb. You'll want to bundle up," he called.

West Thumb is a geyser basin on the shore of Yellowstone Lake. We began to prepare for the outdoors, discussing the types of layers we'd brought to protect ourselves from the cold. Even in temperate seasons, a cool breeze blows off the water, and I dreaded what we would face in deep winter. In spring, summer, and fall, the parking lot bursts with a colorful array of buses, RVs, trucks, SUVs, and cars. On that frosty February day, however, it was an island of white in an evergreen sea, undisturbed and—aside from our snowcoach—empty.

Our driver parked and waited for us to disembark. "If you need to use the comfort station, follow me," he called out.

We waded through the unplowed parking lot toward a small brick building, home to a vault toilet. With no electricity and no plumbing, the only comfort the building provided was a break from the wind and relief from a full bladder. In its heaterless state, the effect of the fifteen-degree air was amplified by the draft that blew through the pit, further chilling the room and assaulting any momentarily bared skin.

With that behind us, we trudged over the snow-packed boardwalk through the geyser basin, a white expanse broken by pools of sapphire and emerald and patches of gray geyserite exposed by the geothermal heat underground. Water flowed from some springs, rivulets carving tiny canyons in the snow.

Our driver knelt down on the boardwalk and pointed. "See that? That over there? It's a fly. And not your ordinary fly. This one's an extremophile—a thermophile, to be more specific. An extremophile is an organism with extreme habitat requirements. A thermophile is an extremophile that requires heat, the kind you find in thermal runoff close to a hot spring or geyser. That's where these guys live."

"These guys" live a precarious existence. If they fly too high or too far from the warmth of the water, they'll die from exposure to the cold. If they fly too low and get too close to the water, they'll die from exposure to the heat.

"As if that's not enough," our driver continued, "they have another danger to contend with: thermophile spiders. While they don't live in the same temperature zone as the flies, the spiders do have the ability to dash from their preferred microclimate over into the flies' turf, catch one for dinner, and dart back to the safety of their own territory."

Hunched against the wintry day, I watched the fly flit about and pondered its perilous life. *How have I never noticed these before?*

After we'd settled back in the snowcoach to resume our journey to the Old Faithful area, Jaime leaned over and as quietly as he could manage with the noise of the engine whispered, "Mason would love this."

I smiled. Yes. Our five-year-old son Mason would love this. The bombardier. The snow. The extremophile flies and spiders. Mostly, though, the bombardier.

8 WILD AND DANGEROUS

We stepped out of our cabin the next morning into a cloud of diamond dust—ambient, sparkling moisture frozen and suspended midair. It's a phenomenon of extremes, requiring conditions to be both cold and still. Strolling through the glistening crystals floating in the new day's sunbeams, our boots squeaked on the undisturbed snow that had fallen in the night. Diamond dust is pure fancy. To pass through it along the way to something as mundane as breakfast was a gift and a delight.

We walked farther than we needed to, taking the long way that would give us a view of the closed-for-the-season Inn. Aside from the buildings and the Upper Geyser Basin's vapor drifting into the day, the serene winter version of the Old Faithful area was nothing like the bustling summer version. Compared to the lineup of cars, trucks, SUVs, and campers of every color wedged into the temperate season's parking lot, the small contingent of monochromatic snowmobiles looked lost and lonely against a sea of sound-absorbing snow. Even the rumbling of the occasional bombardier couldn't lift the morning's heavy silence.

Our day's expedition into the park called for a level of outerwear we did not possess but could rent at the Old Faithful Snow Lodge gift shop. My admiration for my children and the effort they were willing to expend just to play in the snow increased with each piece of cumbersome gear I put on. It hardly seemed worth it, yet I knew from snowmobiling in the park in my teens it was an unavoidable necessity. Deep cold was crucial both to provide and preserve the snow-silenced landscape that drew us to visit Yellowstone in the winter. That level of frostiness combined with wind—whether the naturally occurring variety or the kind created by hurtling down the road at forty-five miles per hour—ushers in a particular brand of misery. The only warmth available to us would come from our own bodies, from occasional warming huts along the way, and from sporadically functioning heaters in the snowmobile's hand grips and footrests. Our gear would harness and hold that heat, protecting us from the penetrating wind.

After a few moments of being marvelously overdressed for the final legal details, it was a relief to step out into the cold for our required snowmobile lesson. A winter's visit nearly twenty years before had started me on my Yellowstone life. Now, uncomfortably hot and knowing I would soon be miserably cold, I was ready to get to know the winter Yellowstone again, this time with Jaime.

After a final reminder that our snowmobile was due back by 4:30 that afternoon, Jaime drove us away from the unfamiliar emptiness of the parking lots and onto the main road, a surface as white and unpopulated as the one we left behind. We headed north, the opposite direction the snowcoach had delivered us from the previous day, toward an area thick with towers of steam rising from the geyser basins that lined the thirty-mile stretch of road between the Old Faithful area and Norris Geyser Basin.

We weren't the first ones out that morning. The previous day's tracks were gone, along with the punishing washboard grooves that continually build up with use. They'd been crushed and redistributed by a snow-grooming machine. Tracks marred the clean corduroy lines left in the groomer's wake, hoof prints from a large mammal on one edge and the tread from a single snowmobile along the other. We hadn't even made it to the nearest geyser basin before we saw the source of the prints: a small herd of bison plodding down the road, more or less single file, in the same direction we were headed.

Snowmobile travel in Yellowstone is confined to official roadways; off-road snowmobiling is not allowed. Oversnow vehicles are subject to the same laws that regulate traffic flow during the rest of the year. This meant we would have to pass the bison. On the road. Within just a few feet—much closer than the park service's twenty-five-yard regulations allowed.

Although I spent my early years on a farm, I have an irrational fear of cows. My uncle, a farmer, once tried to reason me out of it, appealing to the gentleness in their eyes. But it's the eyes that are the problem. Cows hold a long, steady gaze—one that always looks to me as though they may well be calculating whether or not it would be worth the energy to charge the fence and run me down.

Unlike cows, bison do not hold a long, steady gaze. They don't live behind fences. When it comes to running people down, they have an established reputation.

When we reached the herd, Jaime paused for a moment, then put a little pressure on the accelerator. I tightened my grip on his waist and tried not to breathe or do anything else that might draw the attention of the bison. They were a small bunch—only half a dozen. Still, between our slow speed and my intense fear, it took an eternity to get from the first to the last.

The road followed the Firehole River. Warmed by the thermal runoff that pours into it as it runs through five geyser basins, the waterway is often shrouded in steam. Between the river and the road—far enough away that I could enjoy them—small herds of bison sought their daily bread, each one working its immense brown head back and forth like a bucket on an excavator to expose the frozen vegetation beneath. *What a way to forage for an unsatisfying lunch*, I thought as we passed.

About six miles down the road, we stopped at Midway Geyser Basin. We dismounted and clomped across the wooden bridge, making our way through the blinding mist created by the four thousand gallons of scalding runoff that flowed every minute from Excelsior Geyser Crater, down the hill, and into the Firehole River. Frozen steam glazed the packed snow on the boardwalk, and we joked that Jaime, who started playing hockey when he was seven, would have navigated it more easily in skates than boots. Had Midway not been Jaime's favorite geyser basin, I would have turned back. When we made it the thirty treacherous yards up the slope to the plateau, we faced an even thicker haze. The vapor veil lifted only occasionally, revealing the boardwalk and inciting unsettling visions of a misstep off and subsequent plunge into one of Midway's thermal features. With Jaime's hand clamped around mine, we circled the basin, collecting condensation on our faces, hats, and snowmobile suits, and seeing little but a cloud of steam.

We were barely out of the parking lot when we passed a white sign with bold red letters:

CAUTION BISON
ARE WILD AND
DANGEROUS
DO NOT APPROACH

That much I knew. What I didn't know was how we were supposed to not approach them when we were both traveling the same road. Bison frequently took the packed and groomed road, probably because it requires less energy. Wading through deep snow expends much of the limited fuel bison have available to survive the winter—fuel that comes more from the fat they store during the summer and fall than from the food they forage for during winter. Our snowcoach driver told us he'd heard a park biologist compare a bison's diet to a box of cereal. During the growing season, they eat the cereal. During the winter, they eat the box.

Even though they look to be slowly starving during the winter months, bison are massive. When grown, a female can weigh a half-ton and a male a full ton. The ones we'd passed that morning were a mixed group of females, yearlings, and the previous spring's calves—along with young bulls who had not yet left the herd. They were big enough. Intimidating, too, as they traveled alongside our snowmobile, appropriately wild looks in their eyes —eyes which were uncomfortably level with my own.

We joined a line of snowmobiles making their slow, deliberate way past another small band of bison. A young male in the middle of the herd began to trot as Jaime started to pass him. Jaime slowed down. The bison slowed down. Jaime sped up. The bison sped up.

The words of a ranger we'd once chatted with at Grant Village rang in my head: "I worked with Kodiak bears in Alaska, and I'm more wary of bison than bears. Bison are irritable and unpredictable." This one fit that description, and I was certain we were going to be killed. Or at least gored. Unlike the snowcoach, our snowmobile didn't provide any actual protection. Bison are not only unpredictable; they're fast—up to thirty miles per hour fast —and, reputedly, grumpy. After a couple more rounds of speeding up and slowing down, Jaime passed the young bison, and we emerged, uncharged and ungored.

Free from the herd, Jaime hung back a little to put some space between us and the other snowmobiles. Before long, he pointed into the distance without saying anything. Of the few things Jaime does that annoy me, this tops the list. On the snowmobile, of course, he couldn't help it. He couldn't easily say, "Hey, look at the ... "

Communication was limited, so I tried to be patient. I tried to not grumble. I searched for what might have caught his attention. Was it a snow formation? A bear? A bison? An elk? Some lovely thing I wouldn't think to look for? I knew it would be worth seeing, but what it might be was a mystery.

I saw nothing on the ground. Nothing on the river. Nothing in the trees. Finally, I found it—a bald eagle soaring directly overhead.

Jaime stopped beside the Firehole, turned off the engine, and took off his helmet. "Did you find it?" he asked "Did you see the eagle?"

I took off my helmet and nodded, contrite that I'd grumbled when he was sharing something lovely. We settled in to watch the eagle as it circled overhead, searching the river for a trout. When it landed in a tree on the far bank, I thought Jaime might want to leave. I prepared to put on my helmet, but he didn't move, so I stopped. With nothing to do other than watch what he wanted to watch and no deadline other than our 4:30 p.m. snowmobile curfew, he was free to sit by the water and watch Yellowstone being Yellowstone and the eagle being an eagle. And so was I.

Aside from the river, Yellowstone was still and, aside from its head, so was the eagle. Eventually, it dropped from its perch, caught some wind, and rose into the air. We stayed, wrapped in Yellowstone's plush winter blanket, admiring the eagle and absorbed by the park's vast solitude and our small place in it.

"Do you want to drive?" Jaime asked when we were ready to move on.

I shook my head. I did not want to be at the helm if we ran into any more bison. Naturally, almost as soon as we got to full speed, that's exactly what happened.

It was another small herd, but bison are bison, and I kept envisioning the sign I'd seen earlier that morning:

CAUTION BISON
ARE WILD AND
DANGEROUS
DO NOT APPROACH

Even as I silently willed Jaime to turn around and return to the lodge where the only bison were decorative, I knew I didn't want to give up and go back. Not really.

When Jaime slowed and pulled over to the farthest possible edge of the road, I tried to turn my head and not watch them as we passed. But I couldn't resist. I eyed them from my open seat and wished for a vehicle with proper doors.

I had no recollection of bison on the road back when I'd been here with my family fifteen years before. I could have blocked it out. It would have been traumatic enough. More likely, though, it was that there were fewer bison. That had been during the winter of 1986-87, when the herd numbered less than three thousand. In the intervening years, that number had grown by a thousand. Plus, at eighteen, I probably held the belief that teenagers and young adults are reputed to have, the one that makes us think we'll live forever, that we're impervious to danger, destruction, and death. Now I was thirty-three and knew better. Aches and pains made it abundantly clear the only way I'd live forever would be in whatever kind of new body God would outfit me with when this life was over. Passing by those bison, I couldn't ignore my mortality.

In less time than it seemed, we were safely past the herd and on our way to Norris Junction. In the empty parking lot, we took off our helmets and trudged toward Norris's Back Basin. Away from the road, even one as untaken as a Yellowstone winter road, the sculpted landscape further stilled and silenced the air around it. Our boots squeaked with every heavy step we took over snow packed hard by the few who had walked the path before us. We were there for Echinus Geyser, a family favorite. Its predictable, short, showy cycle meant we'd be able to tell if we'd just missed an eruption or if we'd be waiting a while. Either way, it wouldn't be long until the next one. Echinus's eruption cycle begins with the gradual filling of the large, bowl-shaped depression in which it sits —eventually spilling over the top and flowing down the slope, under the boardwalk, and into the central basin beyond.

When we arrived, Echinus's crater had already started to fill. Estimating we had about a half hour before the eruption, we took our solitary seats on bleachers a few yards away from the geyser's center. While we were alone in terms of human companionship, we were in company with another small herd of bison. Half a dozen of them had settled themselves on the ground on the other side of Echinus, far enough off they didn't scare me.

Unlike humans who, by law, must keep to the boardwalk in thermal areas, animals can go wherever they want. It doesn't always end well. Bleached skeletal remains of large mammals resting on the bottom of the occasional hot spring attest to that. They're drawn, I suppose, by the heat of the earth and the enveloping steam. I'd always wondered, when I saw them gathered near a thermal feature, parked on a patch of warm earth, wearing hoarfrost in their fur like a crusty suit of armor, exactly what they did in the event of an eruption.

I was about to find out.

Some sat on the snowless ground, their legs tucked primly beneath their bulky bodies. Others stood in the rising steam. They didn't react to the filling bowl or the thickening mist. They didn't move when the water spilled over the rim and down the slope. The eruption was close. I knew it. But I never looked away from the bison. I was more interested in their response to the eruption than in the eruption itself. Would they sit there? Would they run? Had they known to choose a spot far enough away that they wouldn't get splashed by the scalding water?

When Echinus erupted, sending explosive bursts of superheated water and steam into the sky, the bison didn't just sit there. Neither did they run or dart or even scurry away. They simply hoisted their immense bodies off the earth and lumbered out of the water's reach. When it was over, they returned to their places.

After years of wondering what bison did in the face of an eruption, I had an answer. They moved. That's it. They did what they needed to do, when they needed to do it. Then they returned to their place and their business, which, that day, was surviving the cold.

I could learn a thing or two from that.

9 SHARING THE ROAD

Aside from the absence of diamond dust, the next morning unfolded the same as the first. After bundling ourselves into our snowmobile suits and donning our helmets, we took off in the same direction as the day before. We hadn't gone far before we came upon a line of six snowmobiles stopped on the road. Bison again. The largest herd we'd encountered yet.

My stomach twisted in a now-familiar fashion, and I reinforced my grip around Jaime's waist. Two dozen bison of varying sizes ambled along ahead of us. They were going our way, taking up more than their share of the road for a good half-mile stretch. We took our place at the end of the string of snowmobiles and waited our turn to risk death by goring. At regular intervals, the snowmobile that was next in line would accelerate and set out alone on the long passage from one end of the herd to the other.

What are we doing? I thought, recalling the sign we'd seen the day before. *Bison are wild and dangerous.*

The road was the only way to get from where we were to where we wanted to be, and already I was worn from sharing it with bison. I kept hoping the head bison in every little herd would decide that they'd arrived at wherever they were going, make a sharp turn, and lead the whole herd off into the shoulder-deep snow—leaving us free to carry on without risking our lives every few miles. My anxiety increased with each snowmobile that left its place of relative security behind the herd to begin the perilous journey to the temporarily bison-free zone on the other side. Slowly, the number of snowmobiles ahead of us dwindled down to three, then two, then one. Then it was just us. *Don't go. Don't go. Don't go.* I pled silently, even though I didn't want to turn around. Not really. I didn't want to give in to fear. I didn't want to retreat to the imagined safety of the indoors.

We were here to snowmobile. I wanted to snowmobile. I just wished we didn't have to share the road.

Jaime accelerated lightly and eased our machine toward the herd. We passed the first, second, and third animals—all trotting along, head down, one wild eye always trained in our direction. I watched them out of the corner of my own eye, once again wishing for a proper vehicle with doors to lock and windows to roll up. At home, I was uncomfortable this close to a cow even with a barbed wire fence between us. And here I was, only a few feet from a bison, far closer than I would consider approaching on the trail. We passed the fourth, fifth, and sixth bison and I relaxed—a little. But as we approached number seven, a big one, he pivoted into our path.

It was over. I knew it. We were going to be gored, trampled, and left alone on the side of the snow-packed road to die.

Except, when the snowmobile in front of us reached the end of the herd, the woman in the passenger seat turned around. She must have seen us because she pounded on the driver's back until their vehicle slowed, at which point she switched to gesturing wildly in our direction until the driver stopped. They could do nothing to help us, yet I took comfort in knowing she'd seen us and they'd waited. We might still get gored, but at least we weren't alone.

I tapped Jaime on the shoulder and lifted my helmet's face shield. "What are we gonna do?" I asked, as loudly as I dared.

"Wait," he answered.

"Wait for what?"

"To see what he does, I guess."

"Is there somewhere we can go?" I asked.

"No. We can't back up, and we can't turn around."

"Maybe the ditch or behind the snowmobile where he won't have his face so close to us?" I continued, desperate.

"No." Jaime covered my hands with one of his. "We stay on the snowmobile, Nat. On the snowmobile."

Unable to face the wild and dangerous animal staring us down and intimidated by his stillness, his size, and his steamy breath, I closed my eyes and flattened myself against Jaime's back, trying—without success—to block out the words circling like vultures in my brain: *more wary of bison than bears ... wild and dangerous ... irritable and unpredictable ... do not approach.*

With all that swirling in my head, I snuck a look at the rest of the herd as it made its slow-motion way past us over the freshly groomed snow. Turning away, I surveyed what I could see of the landscape on the other side and wished for a way out. Seeing none, I peeked over Jaime's shoulder, where the big boy still held his ground inches from our windshield, occasional puffs of his frozen breath rising before us. Certain we faced imminent goring, I buried my head behind Jaime's back again and vacillated between despair over our probable death and prayer that the bison would move out of our way.

He did.

In the same sudden and unexpected way he'd swung into our path, he swiveled back out and fell in step with his brethren. With him out of the way, Jaime squeezed the accelerator, and—with more urgency and speed than usual—put the big bison and the rest of the herd behind us. Up ahead, the woman who'd waited while we faced the bison waved. I waved back, grateful for her presence on the wild, winter road.

We hadn't been alone. And I had seen another Yellowstone miracle.

"Do you have everything you need?" Jaime asked the next day after lunch.

I'd settled into a wing chair next to the fireplace in the Snow Lodge, a stack of books by my side.

"Yep."

"You sure?"

Jaime always feels a twinge of guilt when he heads out into the park without me. He forgets that I lived in this place, and to sit and read a book, to walk the Upper Geyser Basin boardwalk, to catch yet another eruption of Old Faithful is to revisit an old and beloved life. And magnificent though Yellowstone's winter may be, restorative as its silence is, I was done with the solitude of its road for a while. I was ready to be in the company of humans rather than forced into close quarters with bison.

I was sure.

At least, I was sure until several hours later when the sky intruded on my bison-free afternoon by taking on the melancholy look it gets before it gives up the sun. I checked my watch and the window. Three o'clock. The view beyond the buildings and Old Faithful was Jaime-less. More than that, it was people-less. Not a single person stirred on the sidewalk in the flat light of the afternoon sun. Jaime had gone out to snowshoe the Upper Geyser Basin, a long haul over a clear boardwalk in temperate seasons. That day, nearly a foot of fresh powder covered winter's snowpack. It would take him a while.

I told myself not to fret. It was cold but not brutal. Jaime was dressed for it. He was young and healthy and resourceful. He wasn't in the backcountry alone or on the road with bison. He was, however, mostly alone on a snow-covered boardwalk, spending a peaceful day in a wild place where there are all kinds of ways to die. Ways—aside from bears—I didn't usually dwell on. I knew I didn't need to worry—yet. I knew I shouldn't worry at all. But it was becoming a habit. So I stuck with *yet*—I didn't need to worry yet. I decided to wait until four o'clock. Even as I set my deadline, I knew it was a bad idea. *Who sets a time for starting to worry?*

I heard him before I saw him, his distinctive, quick step coming my way. He'd arrived between my surreptitious glances toward the Old Faithful area's buildings and the geyser basin beyond. His face shone as he crossed the lobby toward my seat by the fire. Jaime's a smiler, but this was different. He glowed—relaxed, happy, and whole—restored by a few peaceful hours in the wilderness.

Sometimes that's all it takes and—bison, bears, and worry aside—that's why we were there.

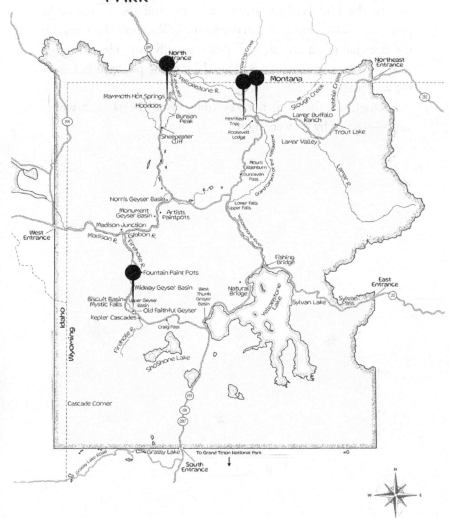

10 BEAR-FIGHTING STICK

The smell of chlorine hung in the hotel corridor like the sulfur haze over a geyser basin.

"Can we swim?" Mason asked.

"Yeah. Can we swim? Please?" Elyse echoed.

"It's late. I'm sure the pool is closed. We'll swim in the morning," I told them.

Unfortunately, the path to our room took us past the still-open pool and the sign posting its hours of operation. It closed at midnight. Jaime and I looked at each other over Mason and Elyse's heads. He'd had a long day of driving. I was three months pregnant. We were ready for bed. But the kids loved to swim.

Jaime smiled. "Better change fast. The pool closes in twenty minutes."

Mason and Elyse were awake and whispering before six the next morning. Like me, both kids were early risers, especially when they were excited. And they were excited. The pool opened at six and, thanks to the sign, they knew it. Jaime and I forced ourselves out of bed and shepherded them to the pool, to breakfast, and back to the pool. We were showered and in the van by a quarter to ten for the final half of the drive—from Spearfish, South Dakota, to Yellowstone's east gate—just as we'd planned.

After spending the night at Mammoth Hot Springs, we drove the winding road five miles north to Gardiner so the kids could see the Roosevelt Arch, an imposing stone structure with eight words chiseled across the top:

> FOR THE BENEFIT AND
> ENJOYMENT OF THE PEOPLE

The monument's name honors President Theodore Roosevelt, not so much for his support of national parks, but because he happened to be vacationing in the park when the arch was dedicated. The words come from the 1872 act of Congress that brought Yellowstone into existence, setting apart a "tract of land... as a public park or pleasuring-ground for the benefit and enjoyment of the people."[1] While no one, aside from park employees, can live there, it's open to anyone who wants to visit and available to everyone who, like me, finds in it a home.

Just a few miles inside the entrance, Jaime pulled into a small lot. We piled out and crossed the road to walk the flat mile to Boiling River, one of few places in Yellowstone where it's legal to swim or soak in thermal runoff.[2] A distant hot spring flows into the Gardner, and people come year-round to experience the warm, mineralized waters downstream. Steam rose from the river as we walked through the crisp morning air.

It was May. Thanks to the late-spring weather debacle Jaime and I experienced two years into our marriage, I had accepted that May in the mountains differed from the one we'd left behind in

---

1. On March 1, 1872, Yellowstone was established by the Yellowstone National Park Protection Act. The phrase on the arch is anchored in a string of legal language that gives the park its purpose, making it a place "reserved and withdrawn from settlement, occupancy, or sale" and providing "for the preservation ... of all timber, mineral deposits, natural curiosities, or wonders." It's a big job. Thanks to the internet, the text of the act can be found by searching "Yellowstone protection act."
2. Because the floods of 2022 washed out several stretches of road in the north end of the park, as of this writing, Boiling River is neither accessible by road nor open for swimming or soaking.

Iowa. We were all appropriately clad for the weather in jeans, jackets, hats, and mittens. We arrived to find a small group of soakers, and even though it looked fun, I didn't envy them the chill they would experience upon exiting the water. While most of them sat without moving, their shoulders submerged below the surface, one woman busied herself scooping mineral-rich mud from the bottom of the river and slathering it on every bit of her exposed skin. Mason and Elyse stood wide-eyed on the river bank and, for once, did not ask to swim.

"Grr."

"Where are the kids?" I asked, busy with the sandwiches I was making for lunch.

Jaime looked up from the pack he was preparing for our hike. "They were just here," he said. More fierce sounds erupted from behind the boulder Mason and Elyse had been standing on moments before. Jaime set down the pack.

"What are you guys up to?" he asked, walking in the direction of the growls.

They popped out from behind the boulder, Mason brandishing a stick. "We're practicing fighting bears," he said.

"This is our bear-fighting stick," Elyse added.

A bear-fighting stick? I shook my head and gave Jaime a look. Maybe he could make them understand.

He knelt down so he was at their eye level. "Hey guys, bears aren't something we fight. Bears are something we want to avoid."

They looked at him and nodded. Watching from my spot at the picnic table, I hoped they got the message.

After lunch, we set off under a solid gray sky on one of our favorite short trails in the park. I'd first hiked it when Mom and Dad spent just *under* forty-eight hours on the road to spend just *over* forty-eight hours with me during the summer I worked at

Old Faithful. It had been a warm, sunny July afternoon, and the slopes wore a carpet of wildflowers.

With its uninspiring name, the Yellowstone River Picnic Area Trail conjures images of something one could conquer in flip-flops while pushing an umbrella stroller. It isn't. Rising steadily up a lightly wooded slope, it passes a massive boulder before snaking precariously along the edge of the Grand Canyon of the Yellowstone. Perhaps its name offers an advantage; rarely do we encounter other hikers.

A few feet up the trail, we paused to remind the kids to stay close. Elyse looked at us with disbelief that her parents could be so forgetful.

"But we have our stick," she said in her little singsong voice.

The stick again. Elyse and Mason had practiced, and they were ready to fight.

Most of us who enter bear country have only a vague notion of what we're getting into. Kids have less. Unlike me, our children had no fear of bears—perhaps because Yellowstone was something they'd known from their infancy. It had never been alien or mysterious to them. While Jaime continued the work of teaching them what they needed to know about bears and bear protocol, I prayed for a bear-free hike.

"Hiking is a lot of work," Elyse said as we made our way up the slope.

She was right. Procuring and packing supplies and gear, strengthening our knees at home to avoid injury on the trail, and finding the right hikes—these all take time and energy. And then there are all the extras that come with navigating the whole thing with kids. It is a lot of work. But it's worth it. Since our children won't grow up living in the mountains, we want them to grow up with the mountains alive in them.

Hard or not, Elyse kept at it and, even with all the talk of the bear-fighting stick, she and Mason climbed the final slope in step with Jaime. At the top, we didn't need the trail guide's warning to keep a firm hand on our children. That came instinctively, to all of us. Hand in hand, we studied the Yellowstone River snaking between the steep forested walls as we trekked along the ridge.

We hadn't been there long when Jaime told us we'd better turn around. He pointed at the sky, where solid gray had given way to churning clouds. Soon after we reversed course, it started to sprinkle. Hunched against the unwelcome precipitation, we walked faster—as fast as a family with a four-year-old could walk. A cold wind came in with the rain, blowing away the protective micro-climate created by our bodies and reminding me how fragile humans are without the benefit of shelter or proper clothing.

My dad had tried to teach me to pay attention to the weather. Not long after I moved to Yellowstone, he mailed me his well-worn copy of *Yellowstone Trails*, along with a list of hikes he recommended.[3] He ended with this fatherly admonition:

> *Please remember to observe all the precautions mentioned in the book—even in the summer, you are in more danger from hypothermia than from bears. Be careful and have fun. Love—Dad*

Jaime, who is always more prepared for a potential turn in the weather than I am, produced hats and mittens from his pack and distributed them among us. Before long, the rain changed to snow and we slowed again, not because we had to but because we wanted to. Of the things Mason wanted to do that week, "climb a snowy mountain" topped the list, and now we were.

The spring snow wasn't unheard of, but it was unexpected. It wasn't miraculous, but it was a gift, a small grace that brought two kids—and their parents—joy. Protecting and providing. This

---

3. This hiking guide is still in print and is included in the Resources and Reading section at the end of this book.

is what fathers do, seeing not only to what we need in the wilderness but also to what we want.

11 DANGEROUS GROUND

In typical fashion, Mason and I woke the next morning a little before Elyse and long before Jaime. After everyone was up, we set off into the quiet Mammoth Hot Springs community. We took the long way to the Albright Visitor Center, walking past the rows of houses built by the Army back when it served as Yellowstone's steward. Today, Mammoth is park headquarters. In the late eighteen and early nineteen hundreds, it was Fort Yellowstone—base of operations for the Army's oversight of the park's 2.2 million acres of wilderness, thermal features, waterfalls, and wild animals, along with the accompanying poachers, squatters, and unruly tourists. Some of the original Army structures still stand, the building that houses a visitor center, homes on Officer's Row, and a chapel among them.

Today's park rangers both educate and enforce the law. They drive the roads to manage wildlife-induced traffic jams. They walk the boardwalks to talk with the interested and redirect the errant. They do evening programs and take desk duty at the visitor centers.

While conversation on the boardwalk can unfold in a thousand different ways, my time at the Old Faithful Visitor Center taught me that desk conversations are often predictable. After answering the same questions again and again, all season long, it takes effort to remember that while the question may be old to you, it's new to the person standing across the desk. Most rangers, most of the time, do a remarkable job of remembering this and bringing excitement to helping people navigate the park and plan their visit.

The ranger working the desk at the Albright Visitor Center that day did exactly that. After answering our questions, he asked about our plans for the day. "Oh," he said. "It sounds like you have time to stop at Petrified Tree. You should always go there because you might see a moose, but you should especially head over there now. A black bear's been hanging around below the road."

We decided to follow his advice. First, though, we made our final stop in the Mammoth Hot Springs area: the springs themselves.

Because this area lacks the vivid colors and drama of gushing water and roaring steam of the geyser basins in the interior of the park, visitors often think Mammoth's springs are dying—or already dead. In reality, the lack of color isn't the absence of life but evidence of the changing nature of it. The springs flow in different places at different times, carrying mineral-rich thermal water from below the ground, depositing it on the surface and causing the terraces to glow with a watercolor wash over a fresh coat of limestone. Gray areas aren't dead. They're dormant. Still, it's hard to remember that these colorless places once sparkled in the sunlight. These cliffs were active once and may yet be again, a living testament that all things are beautiful in their time.

As sometimes happens at Old Faithful, people miss what is because of what is not. Because the entirety of Mammoth's terraces aren't frosted peach, cream, and ochre—a layered dessert served up for quick consumption—visitors often pass it by. This makes Mammoth a comparatively quiet place, a reprieve from the crowds.

After parking in a tight spot on the plateau above the terraces,

Jaime, the kids, and I approached the boardwalk, passing by a sign:

Dangerous Ground

With its white letters highlighted against the familiar red banner, it reminded me there are countless ways to die in Yellowstone. Some of these could happen just as easily at home. Others—hypothermia, slipping into the canyon, falling into a geyser, being attacked by a bear, and getting gored by a bison among them—are more specific to the wilderness, Yellowstone's wilderness in particular. Below the initial warning, the sign went on—in five different languages:

> "In thermal areas the ground may be a thin crust above boiling hot springs or scalding mud. There is no way to guess a safe path: New hazards can bubble up overnight and some pools are acidic enough to burn through boots. More than a dozen people have been scalded to death and hundreds badly burned and scarred. Leaving the boardwalk or trail, or taking pets beyond this point, is unlawful and potentially fatal."

At the bottom was a drawing of a boy, off the boardwalk and alone, in the process of breaking through the thin crust into steaming water below. I'd seen the sign before. It's plastered all over the thermal areas to save the unaware, the foolish, and the distracted from themselves, and a sad reminder of a child who had actually met such an end.

While we had no plans to leave the boardwalk, the soft lines of Mammoths's sorbet-smudged algae mats remade themselves in my mind. Misty pastel pools morphed into a massive steaming cauldron of death, one that Jaime and I were leading our children toward. We'd had the kids here before, back when they were small and safe in our arms. This was different. Now they were free agents of sorts, walking on their own.

Why would any sane person do this? I asked myself.

Like Jaime had done the day before at the Yellowstone Picnic Area, I knelt down at the kids' eye level. Pointing toward the sign, I said, "It's important to stay on the boardwalk. The ground here is really thin, and there's boiling hot water underneath. You could fall through and get burned. You need to hold Mom or Dad's hand." They looked back, solemn eyes as big as the moon.

I could have stopped.

I should have stopped.

They were smart. And although they might pretend to fight bears with a stick, they weren't prone to running about, willy-nilly. But kids are impetuous, and I felt compelled to continue. "You know how when we make macaroni and cheese, the pasta is hard and crunchy when we put it in the boiling water and it turns soft when it cooks? Well, if our bodies fall into boiling water ... "

"Hey, guys! Look at that!" Jaime broke in, pointing at some imaginary thing behind the kids. He didn't say anything but he shot me a clear *You have got to be kidding* look over their heads.

He was right. I knew it without being told. I needed to worry less and trust more—and trust in something better than the logic of pathetic pasta analogies. That had been so much easier to manage before the kids had taken to walking about on their own. With a sigh, I pasted a smile on my face, took Elyse's hand, and joined Jaime and Mason on the boardwalk to danger and death.

12 PUSHING BOUNDARIES

"But how will we find any bears?" Elyse wailed.

Jaime, Mason, and I already had our bear bells, but when we stopped at the Hamilton Store in Mammoth Hot Springs to buy one for Elyse, they were out of stock.[1]

"Bear bells don't help us find bears, Girlie," I said. "They help us to not surprise bears. They jingle when we walk, and the noise tells them they aren't alone."

That was the theory, anyway. If a bear hears a human—or a group of them—approaching, it will be less likely to be startled and, therefore, less likely to be aggressive. Sharp sounds such as shouting or clapping are most effective, and talking is always helpful. Some people think bears have become acclimated to the sounds of bells. Still, they're a good reminder to make some noise. Silence on the trail is dangerous.

From the store, Mason read the map and we followed his directions to the Petrified Tree area, as the ranger suggested. Old photographs show the petrified remains of three trees but, thanks

---

1. Today these shops are the Yellowstone General Stores. Because the Hamilton Stores were known as Ham stores when I first visited the park and for decades before and after, they may remain so forever in my mind.

to the diligent efforts of souvenir seekers, only one remains. Not surprisingly, it is now secured behind a black wrought-iron fence.[2]

"There it is!" Mason shouted from the back seat.

This was no semi-visible distant dark spot that someone said was a bear. This was a bear exactly as I wanted to see one, engrossed in the business of daily life, safely remote and seemingly oblivious to our presence. As soon as Jaime parked in the little lot near the small gathering of observers, we crossed the single lane to join them. After a few minutes, I sat down on the road's slim shoulder and dangled my legs over the edge so I could more comfortably watch the bear nosh his way through the steep-sided meadow below.

"When are we going down?" Elyse asked from her seat beside me.

"Down where?" I asked, absentmindedly.

Looking at me with something like pity—as though I was the child and she, the patronizing adult—she pointed at the brown back peeking over the top of May's emerging grass. "Down there. To see the bear."

This was the bear she'd wailed over that morning, the one she was sure we wouldn't find. Now that we'd found it she wanted to see it and, apparently, distance would not do. Because she understood neither a bear's nature nor its power, it made sense to her that we would go see it up close.

"We're not going down to the bear, Girlie. We're staying up here, where it's safe."

"Are gri'ly bears dangerous?" Elyse asked.

All bears are dangerous.

Black bears, scientifically known as *Ursus americanus*, range through many areas of North America, in heavily wooded areas far from where I live. They aren't always black. They can be brown or cinnamon or even blond. The smaller of the two species

---

2. Aside from some select thermal features and a few deadly drop-offs in frequently visited areas of the canyon, very little in Yellowstone is fenced.

of bears residing in Yellowstone, males generally top out at just over three hundred pounds and females at two hundred. Their curved claws give them good tree-climbing abilities. Grizzlies, or *Ursus arctos horribilis*, are found in Canada, northern Montana, and the greater Yellowstone area. They are named for the grizzled appearance resulting from their white-tipped fur which, like the black bear's, can vary widely in color—from dark brown to cinnamon to blond. Male grizzlies can weigh as much as seven hundred pounds and females as much as four hundred. While their weight makes it difficult to climb trees, they are fast—able to run at speeds of up to thirty miles per hour. Grizzlies have worse reputations than black bears, but both can effect a great deal of damage, even deadly damage, to a full-grown adult.

Park regulations require people to stay twenty-five yards away from most wildlife. For bears and wolves, that distance increases fourfold. When it comes to bears, people seem loath to obey—often succumbing to the urge to edge just a little closer, to try to see just a little bit better. I finally saw my first Yellowstone bear the summer I worked in the park. It was running across a road near Mammoth Hot Springs like a celebrity fleeing a horde of paparazzi, a contingent of camera-wielding tourists at its heels.

It's rare to find a bear jam without an attendant ranger. They're not there to manage the animals. They're there for the crowd—answering questions, establishing boundaries, and reminding the persistent, again and again, to stay back.

But people push boundaries.

Once, when Jaime and I arrived at a traffic-halting bear jam on Dunraven Pass, eighty people were already lined up across both lanes on either side of a thirty-yard gap that two rangers were keeping clear. We joined them, watching and waiting while a grizzly made his excruciatingly slow and winding way up the slope toward the road. As he approached, the crowd pushed against the line the rangers had drawn in the figurative sand, leaning in as far as possible as he passed through the open space between the two sides. Upon reaching the far edge of the road, he walked into the woods, sat down at the base of a pine, and proceeded to scratch his back against the bark. He wasn't far away, but he was hard to see. The rangers worked to control the crowd, telling the headstrong ones again and again, that no, they could not follow the bear into the woods and, no, they couldn't move any closer.

And then it happened. A tall, beefy man crossed the line and stepped into the clearing to take a picture. The ranger closest to him—a petite woman—sprinted his way, collared him, and shoved him back over the line and into the side of his truck. "What part of *get back* did you not understand?" she shouted. By the time her imposing counterpart was by her side, the man and the unruly members of the crowd had gotten themselves under control.

Maybe we all need fences. Because, when it comes to bears, it isn't only children who don't understand.

13 WHY WORRY?

"Is that a wolf?" Mason asked, putting down his map and pointing at a buff-colored canine ambling along in a meadow.

Whatever it was, it was habituated. As soon as Jaime pulled off the road, it turned and trotted directly toward us. Mason and Elyse unbuckled so they could get a good view, moving from window to window and watching as the animal circled our vehicle, occasionally looking directly at us. After some study, we decided that, while it was large, it lacked a wolf's bulk and shoulder angle, so it must be a coyote. We watched until he trotted off. When Jaime pulled back onto the road to continue our journey from the Petrified Tree and the bear, it wasn't long before we found ourselves traveling through a heavy spring snow, the squall still visible in the rearview mirror after we emerged.

We arrived at Old Faithful to find a rapidly emptying boardwalk. Since we'd just missed an eruption, we set off for a long, winding walk through the Upper Geyser Basin. Having made it through Mammoth Hot Springs with the kids intact, I was able to worry a little less and enjoy the mysteries of the stark, steamy landscape a little more. We took the boardwalk at the kids' pace, past hissing fumaroles and bubbling pools. As we walked, we looked at geysers of all shapes and sizes interspersed with sporadic stands of lodgepole pines, many of them stunted by the basin's hostile growing conditions. In a couple of places, we found ourselves near the Firehole River as it flowed through, collecting thermal runoff along the way.

Unlike other thermal features, Riverside Geyser deposits its water directly into the Firehole. It looked close to eruption when we reached it, evidenced by water spilling and sometimes surging from its cone. This timing was a gift. While Riverside is predictable, because more than six hours pass between eruptions, we didn't often see it erupt. Situated on the gently sloping riverbank, it is unusual in that it does not erupt upward. Rather, the eruption arcs at an angle across the water. This—when conditions are right, as they were on that afternoon—sometimes creates a rainbow. Lingering, we watched it bow gracefully over the river.

From there, we walked to Morning Glory Pool at what felt like the end of the road. As lovely as the name implies yet less magnificent than it used to be, years of park visitors taking more than pictures and leaving more than footprints have taken a toll. The delicate scallop-edge that once lined the pool is gone, and its vivid, morning glory blue has faded. While the scallops—deposits of the mineral geyserite, or sinter—simply went for souvenirs, the color change is more complex. Coins and other random items people feel compelled to throw into pools—even miraculous thermal ones—have changed the way water flows into and through Morning Glory. This has cooled the water and created the right conditions for thermophiles to take up residence. Today, orange and yellow organisms thrive along the edge that the scallops once decorated.

Still, Morning Glory was a worthwhile destination. Unfortunately, its location at the end of the long, looping Upper Geyser Basin boardwalk made for a lengthy haul back to the Inn, especially for little legs.

"Keep walking, Elyse," Jaime urged.

"I am, Daddy. Can't you see my feet moving?" she answered, pointing at her shoes and shuffling in an exaggerated manner.

Jaime swung her up on his shoulders and carried her down the long path back to the Upper Geyser Basin's main trail, where we could see steam rising from the area of Castle Geyser. We picked up our pace. This was something we didn't want to miss. Judging from the size of the gathering crowd, we'd arrived just in time for the hour-long event that is a Castle eruption. Knowing we would be there a while, we found an open space on a bench and sat down to wait. Castle eruptions are not only predictable—at that time occurring about every twelve hours—they're showy. For fifteen minutes, superheated water surged to heights of seventy five feet from its castle-shaped cone, followed by a roaring steam phase reminiscent of a locomotive engine.[1]

"Can we come back and see this again?" Mason asked as we walked away. While he was a keen observer of small things, he also loved trains and all things large. Castle, because of the magnitude of its eruption and the size of its cone, became an immediate favorite.

The next morning we traveled south toward Yellowstone Lake, just to drive and see what we would see. Three months pregnant and easily worn out, I was glad for the time in the van. Fortunately for me, a Yellowstone vacation is a driving vacation. Of the nearly three thousand miles we put on our vehicle each time we visit the park, a third come from driving from one place to another within its borders.

Not far beyond the Old Faithful area, we began the climb to Craig Pass. At the continental divide, we stopped to snap a photo of ourselves—uncoated and shivering—next to the sign still partially buried in the deep snow piled on the shoulder. We stopped again, this time at the Shoshone Lake Overlook for a view

---

1. Geysers erupt from a variety of formations. Some erupt from a pool, some from little more than a hole in the ground, and others from a cone–a buildup of minerals around the vent.

of Yellowstone's second-largest lake. Jaime and my dad had once taken the twenty-one-mile trek to Shoshone Lake and its remote geyser basin. We'd heard that—on a clear day—it was possible to see the Tetons from the overlook. Alas, it was not a clear day.

Back in the van we continued our journey toward Yellowstone Lake. Not long after the water came into view, Jaime saw a dark figure standing in a small meadow beside the road. "Looks like a moose," he said, pulling off for a closer look.

It was a moose. Big and brown, it wasn't hard to spot among spring's emerging grass. We didn't often see moose, so we stayed a while, passing Jaime's binoculars around while we watched the large mammal placidly eating its breakfast.

At the intersection, Jaime turned toward the lakeshore and then again at the West Thumb Geyser Basin. After we'd donned coats and hats for the omnipresent chilly breeze blowing off the water, we set off down the boardwalk. Named for its location on what resembles a thumb attached to Yellowstone Lake, West Thumb Geyser Basin is unlike others in the park. Not only is it located directly on the shoreline, a few of its features are actually in the water—including Fishing Cone, where long-ago visitors entertained themselves by catching fish from the lake and then dropping them in the geyser to cook on the line.[2] Other thermal features sit below the surface, their thermal outflow having little effect on the massive body of high-altitude water. Yellowstone Lake never warms enough to swim in safely.

Traveling along the shore, our view was mostly trees. Gaps between the lodgepole trunks shuttered the lake and rugged mountains beyond like an old-style movie. One gap gave us a glimpse of a bear. It was a black bear, loping along the water's edge in the opposite direction. Jaime turned around, found a turnout, and pulled in so we could watch it until it disappeared from sight.

---

2. Cooking in Fishing Cone is no longer allowed for many reasons, including the preservation of the thermal feature and human life.

On our final night in the park, Jaime and I sat on a bench in the falling darkness with the kids on our laps, huddled together for warmth. Castle was predicted to erupt within an hour of eight o'clock, and we'd returned to see it one last time. A splash from its twelve-foot cone caused the crowd to "ooh" and "aah" before settling back into its subdued murmuring. This cycle repeated itself a couple more times—each splash a little higher than the last—until Castle let loose with water that had been trapped below the surface, waiting for release. It surged again and again before abating and giving way to the steam that roared from its cone. When we couldn't take the cold anymore, we left the still-roaring Castle and walked back to the Inn.

Along the way, Mason coughed from somewhere deep in his chest. When we reached the top of the stairs on the second-floor mezzanine, he said, "I don't feel very well."

He was not the first one up the next morning. He stayed in bed while we packed up around him. When we left through the red door, instead of swinging Elyse onto his shoulders, Jaime carried a feverish Mason in his arms. Even though he was sick, Mason got out of the car without complaint at Kepler Cascades, one of two traditional stops we make when we leave through the South Entrance. But as we made our way toward the park border without any of his typical observations or navigational commentary, I worried. This was 2003, the year I first heard of SARS (severe acute respiratory syndrome)—a life-threatening respiratory illness that was reportedly following people out of China. Yellowstone is filled with international tourists, some of them straight from Asia. I worried that he'd crossed paths with someone carrying SARS and was days from death.

When Jaime shut the van off at our second stop, Mason didn't move. Neither did Elyse. I stayed with the kids while Jaime made the pilgrimage to the roadside waterfall alone. After he disappeared from sight, I picked up Mason's park map to occupy myself.

When I was finished, I noted that the people who'd headed to the falls after Jaime departed had already returned to their car and driven away. *What's taking him so long?* I stopped worrying that Mason, and now maybe Elyse, was going to die from SARS and started to wonder if maybe Jaime had sprained an ankle and how in the world could I help him, stuck as I was in the vehicle alone with two sick, sleeping children. By the time I finished going over the map a second time, Jaime's ankle had ceased to be my concern. I was convinced he'd slipped on the snow at the river's edge and plunged over the falls. Because what else would cause a surefooted, wilderness-loving man to linger at his final stop in Yellowstone?

Clearly, my bent toward worry was becoming a problem— and not just in places with posted signs about bears and bison. I worried at home too. Like my tendency to set off on the trail without considering the weather, my habit of worrying about things that were unlikely to happen rather than being ready for the things that were often led me to dangerous ground.

YELLOWSTONE NATIONAL PARK

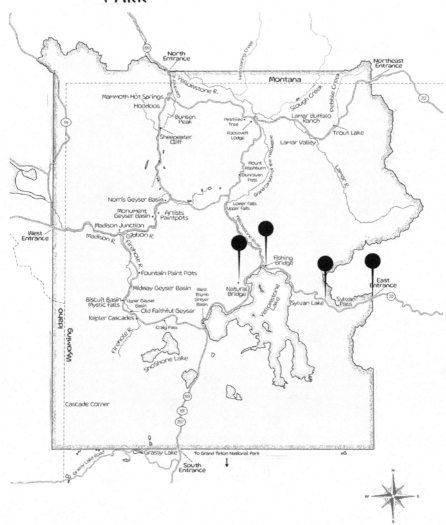

14 ECHOES OF THEIR DAD

"You know the East Entrance closes for the season at ten o'clock tomorrow morning, don't you?" the man behind the counter said when Jaime checked us into our hotel in Cody, Wyoming.

No. We didn't know.

It was September 2004. Emma, the baby we'd been expecting during our visit in May of the previous year, had arrived, and now we were a family of five. In the midst of getting three kids and two adults ready for a trip to Yellowstone, we'd forgotten all about the potential for road-closing construction projects.

The next morning we rose early. We had eight-year-old Mason, five-year-old Elyse, and nine-month-old Emma in and out of the pool, showered, dressed, fed, and buckled into their seats by seven-thirty. Jaime turned toward Yellowstone's East Entrance, just as we'd planned. We could have taken our time and entered the park by the Northeast Entrance through Cooke City and Silver Gate, but we wanted to show the kids places on the east road, so we left early enough to make it.

There are five roads into and out of Yellowstone, each one named for the direction corresponding to its location on the figure-eight roadway, and—no matter if you are coming or going

—attended by a sign bearing the word *entrance*. Whenever we exit the park past an entrance sign, the last line from the Eagles' song "Hotel California" plays in my mind. Yellowstone is technically open year-round. We can go anytime but some of us never leave. In the same way, Yellowstone has never left Jaime or me, and we hope it never leaves our kids.

After an hour of driving through terrain that Theodore Roosevelt called "the most scenic fifty miles in the world," we made it to the East Entrance—long before its ten o'clock closure.

"We're in Yellowstone, Emma," said Elyse in her singsong voice.

Mason added the facts. "You're going to see water fall off of high cliffs and shoot up out of the ground."

"And your eyes will get big and wide!" Elyse finished.[1]

With that established, we paid our twenty-dollar fee and drove in past a sign announcing the elevation: 6,951 feet above sea level. From there, the road climbed fifteen hundred feet over Sylvan Pass. Clinging precariously to the mountainside and cantilevered over nothingness below, its sheer drop-offs are intimidating during temperate seasons. In the winter they are dangerous. The road, groomed for snowcoach and snowmobile travel, is kept open for tourism and to give the year-round employees at Lake access to the outside world. It crosses several avalanche paths. When my family and I snowmobiled this road during my high school years, we came upon a sign letting us know exactly how dangerous Sylvan Pass could be:

---

1. Only in narrating the audio version of *Waking Up in the Wilderness* did I realize Elyse had been quoting Junie B. Jones, the main character from the Junie B. Jones series by Barbara Park. These books were among the many audiobooks we listened to on our cross-country trips to Yellowstone. On that subject, here's some unsolicited advice from those 60,000 miles mentioned back in the prologue: If you road-trip, especially with kids of any age, find yourself some audiobooks to enjoy together along the way.

AVALANCHE
ZONE
NO STOPPING NEXT
ONE MILE.
MAINTAIN - 100 YDS
BETWEEN
VEHICLES.

Even with my youthful belief that I was impervious to death, driving from one edge of that mile to the other felt more terrifying than adventurous, as though it was a gauntlet one of us might not live to pass through again.

We lived—and this day was different. The road was still intimidating, but it was early fall. Avalanches were one thing I didn't need to worry about.

Beyond the pass, Jaime parked in the empty turnout at Sylvan Lake and hopped out of the vehicle, ready to share with Mason and Elyse something of his zeal for rocks and water, trees and fish, how things work and how things live. They were out of the vehicle almost as quickly as Jaime, and the three of them walked straight to the lake.

"Hello!" Jaime shouted up toward the mountains beyond the southern shore.

"*Hello!*" The mountain echoed back.

Jaime and my brother had discovered this spot's perfect echo-producing qualities eight years earlier during a bit of madness my family dubbed the Four-Day Flying Trip, in which six adults and an infant spent forty-eight hours on the road to spend forty-eight in the park. The echo was why we stopped there that morning. Well, that and Jaime's infatuation with water of all kinds.

"Go ahead and try it—there's no one else here," Jaime encouraged the kids.

Their eyes glowed while their little voices called and littler voices answered back. Watching them, the push of the cross-country drive and the pressure to beat the ten o'clock gate closure mingled with the mist from the lake and dissipated into the air. We'd made it.

From Sylvan Lake, we descended deeper into the park, through evergreen woods, past the remnants of burned forest, and eventually to Yellowstone Lake. Less than one thousand feet lower than Sylvan Pass, it is the largest freshwater lake above seven thousand feet in North America. Its high elevation subjects it to the whims of the weather that blows in from the surrounding mountains, and it spends more than half the year frozen.

For the second time in just a few miles, Jaime eased the vehicle into a turnout where an opening between the trees framed a view of the lake and a house-sized rock outcropping a few feet into the water. We got out for a better view and discovered a path. For Jaime and the kids, this was all the invitation they needed. Down the slope to the shore we went. Emma was safe and stable in Jaime's arms, Mason and Elyse scampered ahead, and I made my careful way down. At the bottom, Mason and Elyse raced past two empty picnic tables and stopped at the shore.

"Can we wade?" Mason called back to us.

"Can we?" Elyse echoed. "Please?"

Permission secured, they cast off their shoes and socks and were rolling their pant legs up when Jaime and I reached them. Jaime handed Emma to me, and sat down to do the same. Together they stepped into the icy water and went straight for the rocks. Knowing this would be a long stop, I slipped off my shoes and followed them.

"Mommy and Emma are coming! Mommy and Emma are coming!" Elyse squealed.

"Hang on, Babe. I'll be right there," Jaime said.

I stopped where the water met the outcropping and waited for Jaime and Mason to make their way to us. Jaime took Emma, and Mason reached for my hand to help me over the slick spots below the surface. Once I was situated and stable, Jaime handed Emma back to me and returned to Mason and Elyse.

I first saw Jaime throw a rock two years after we married. He loves to skip stones and throw rocks of all kinds, a love he's shared with our kids. Mason learned to skip rocks at the North Shore of Lake Superior. Elyse's visits to Lake Red Rock in Iowa began before she was even born, the last of those prenatal pilgrimages ending within hours of her birth. Throwing rocks isn't just something Jaime does. It's what they all do.

Jaime held a pebble out to Emma. She reached for it, and he reached for her. She grasped the small stone in her tiny fist while he walked over to the far edge of the outcropping, knelt down, and leaned over the crystal water, several feet below. It was time for her initiation into the family's rock-skipping tradition. I inhaled sharply, ready to protest that this was not a good idea. We were standing on a rock, looking over what felt like a small cliff. The water was deep. And cold. *What are you doing?* I was ready to ask. *What if you trip? What if you fall in? What if you drop her?*

I listened to the words forming in my brain and exhaled. Jaime would not trip. He would not fall. He would not drop her. Balance, my weakness, is his strength. That's why he was the one who carried her down to the lake. That's why he was the one holding her near the water to throw her rock. He was taking care of her. It's what he does.

"Throw it in, Emma," he said. He shook her arm gently at the wrist. "Throw your rock."

Emma uncurled her fingers and dropped her rock. Without a splash, it slipped below the surface. We clapped. Our baby girl had thrown her first rock.

15 COURSE CORRECTIONS

"How ya doing?" Jaime asked me as he retrieved Emma from her car seat at Fishing Bridge.

Two weeks before, while shifting from one foot to the other as I stood in line at a coffee shop, my heel had grazed the wall behind me, twisting my knee and dropping me to the floor. Five days later, after a midnight emergency room visit, an office call, and an MRI, I drowsed in a happy state of semi-consciousness on an operating table in the middle of arthroscopic surgery for a torn meniscus. That is, I drowsed in a happy state until the anesthetist roused me from my medically induced nap.

The surgeon was speaking to me. "It looks like you might be able to hike after all. It's borderline. If I fix it, I'm not sure it will hold. It's up to you. Should I repair it or trim it?"

I struggled to force myself into wakefulness and make sense of his words. Even though he was fully alert and licensed to practice medicine, and I was barely lucid and licensed to teach elementary students, he seemed to be asking me to decide. If he trimmed the tear, I'd walk out of the hospital crutch-free but with a higher likelihood of developing arthritis. If he repaired it, I'd face six weeks on crutches—*if* the repair held, an outcome that seemed to be in question. I had a nine-month-old baby to care for and, far less important but still a factor, we were headed to Yellowstone, and I wanted to hike.

"Just trim it," I said and sank back into slumber.

So, as we followed Mason and Elyse down the sidewalk to Fishing Bridge, Jaime holding Emma in one arm and supporting me with the other, I was more than okay. We were in Yellowstone. Together. And I could hike.

We joined Mason and Elyse a few feet onto the bridge, where they'd stopped to search the river below for trout. Jaime had trained them well.

"Where are the fishermen, Daddy? You said it was a fishing bridge," Elyse asked.

"It's called Fishing Bridge because people used to fish here a long time ago," Jaime explained. "Fishing isn't allowed here anymore, though, because cutthroat trout swim up this river to lay their eggs right around here. It's where the baby fish hatch." He was quiet for a moment, his eyes trained on the water. "Look! There's a trout!"

With that, the three of them were gone—lost in the world below the surface. Fishing Bridge sits only a few yards past where the Yellowstone River flows out of Yellowstone Lake, so I headed to the end of the bridge where a sign read:

> CUTTHROAT TROUT
> SPAWNING GROUND
> DO NOT FISH FROM BRIDGE
> DO NOT FEED FISH

I eased down the stairs and over the sloping banks to the water's edge. Wide and smooth, the river drifted lazily down a peaceful corridor between the trees. It seemed a pleasant enough place for life to begin.

Like some other Yellowstone activities, such as feeding black bears along the road and grizzlies at dumps, harvesting fish here at the spawning grounds started innocently enough. Fishing in Yellowstone was a touristy thing to do. The original bridge was built in the early 1900s, and by the time it was replaced in the 1930s, the design included room for fishermen. Old photos show a solid wall of anglers from one end of the bridge to the other, adults and kids dangling lines into the clear water below.

I heard somewhere it was good fishing. But what was good for the fishermen was bad for the beleaguered cutthroats that had just battled their way upstream over rapids and rocks to do their part to continue the family line. Trout, unlike salmon, do not die after spawning. They can spawn several times in their life—if they can avoid making a lifecycle-ending dining decision at the spawning ground. In time, someone made the connection between the declining trout population and the location of the dangling fishing lines, and that was the end of fishing from Fishing Bridge.

While I'm not as interested in fish as Jaime and the kids are, I thrive in the places trout go about the quiet business of living their lives. I'm happy listening to the melody of the Yellowstone River as I wander down its shore. Creation speaks—more often in a whisper than a shout. Trout waters and their environs help me get still enough to listen.

I appreciate the bridge for what it is today, a standing reminder that when what seemed like a good idea turns out to be a bad one, I am free—maybe even responsible—to change course. At Fishing Bridge, the National Park Service made a course correction that made way for something new. Today people stop simply to look for trout below the surface, and it seems to be enough.

It's enough to keep Jaime and the kids happy for a very long time, anyway, passing Jaime's polarized sunglasses around so they can get a better view of what's happening below the surface. I climbed the stairs, hopeful they were moving toward the vehicle. They weren't, but at least they'd crossed to the other side of the bridge. When I joined them, Jaime handed me his polarized sunglasses so I could more easily find the trout they were watching hold its place behind a small boulder. I watched for a moment before my attention drifted upstream to the mouth of the river, and to Yellowstone Lake beyond. I passed the glasses back. While Jaime and the kids kept searching for trout, I carried Emma back down to the tranquil water.

16 TAKING THE ROAD LESS TRAVELED

Because of my knee surgery, our hiking was limited to flat, non-strenuous trails. Flat trails are hard to find in the mountains, but we pored over our trail guides and found a few, including one we'd never taken before—the trail to Natural Bridge, just a few miles down the road from Fishing Bridge. Sunbeams broke through the canopy of green as we walked the wide path. A service road, it was broad and flat enough to accommodate National Park Service pickup trucks. Mason took the lead with Emma in the jogging stroller, her tiny fists and feathery mohawk waving in the breeze. Elyse alternated between keeping up with her siblings and riding on Jaime's shoulders as we made our way to Natural Bridge through the bright forest.

At a fork in the trail, Mason stopped. "Which way do we go?"

"Either. Both will take us to the bridge." Jaime said as he looked up at Elyse, who was perched on his shoulders. "Do you want to choose the way?" He lifted her over his head and set her down on the ground in front of him.

Elyse walked to where the two trails converged and stood in silence a moment before beginning, "I shall be telling this with a sigh, somewhere ages and ages hence."

We'd begun this little practice about six months before, when we moved across the state of Iowa for Jaime's job. When my parents came to help us settle in, Dad took Elyse out for a walk. Together, they explored our new neighborhood, one filled with curved roads, cul-de-sacs, and misaligned intersections. While they investigated the convoluted sidewalk system that made up our new world, Dad taught her the final stanza from Robert Frost's familiar poem "The Road Not Taken." They stopped at every corner and recited the words together:

> I shall be telling this with a sigh
> Somewhere ages and ages hence:
> Two roads diverged in a wood and I—
> I took the one less traveled by,
> And that has made all the difference.

Then, Dad let Elyse choose which road they would take. They wound their way into new territory, and when they returned she recited her new poem and recounted the adventure of getting lost and finding the way home.

We walked a lot in that neighborhood, and the habit of inviting Elyse to recite her poem and lead the way stuck. Even in Yellowstone, it was natural to let her choose.

It was 2004, and the park's visitation rate was nearing three million people every year. Of those, most kept to the main road, hopping out here and there for a photo. Only a tiny fraction of brave souls applied for permits to camp in the backcountry. Many walked a few stretches of boardwalk or maybe walked them all. Some, like us, spread out over the park's nearly thousand miles of trail.

The roads before us were equally acceptable. One was a continuation of the wide way we were already on; the other was a narrow path into a thicker, darker forest. We'd left our van in the turnout, crossed the busy road, entered the woods, and hadn't seen another human since. Of the two roads before us, both qualified as less traveled.

After reciting her stanza, Elyse stood in silence, considering both paths before turning from the wide, level trail and starting up the narrow incline to the ridge above. The rest of us followed. After a short climb, we came to a flat trail open to the slope on one side and guarded by tightly packed pines on the other. Gone was the bright forest we'd enjoyed earlier. Here the close woods held an air as ominous as an unsanitized fairy tale.

We walked along, her little hand in mine. Looking up at me, she said, "I think this is the road less traveled. Right, Mommy?"

I smiled down at her. "I think so too."

Before long, we reached the trail junction, a T-intersection. From our place on the T's crossbar, we were supposed to turn right. It was a good thing. We couldn't have continued straight if we had wanted to. The way forward was blocked and marked with a sign:

> WARNING
> DUE TO BEAR DANGER
> AREA BEYOND THIS SIGN
> CLOSED
> TO ALL TRAVEL

I shivered. "What should we do? Turn back?"

Jaime pointed right. "Our trail is open. It's the one straight ahead that's closed. There's no reason not to keep going. It's okay."

Sometimes the weight of the wilderness sits more heavily than others. This was one of those times. As much as I worried about bears, sometimes even I managed to forget about their presence. Here, walking as we were on the fringe of a forbidden forest, the sign and its message loomed. Yellowstone is filled with bears, both black and grizzly. The Natural Bridge Trailhead is right across from Yellowstone Lake—prime grizzly habitat. The sign highlighted the likelihood that something clawed and sometimes carnivorous lurked in the adjacent, unfenced woods. It occurred to me that, left to my own devices, I was not exactly as secure in my place at the top of the food chain as Mr. Hamel's eighth-grade science class had led me to believe. We carried bear spray, of course, but it hardly seemed enough.

With Natural Bridge not far down the path, I trudged on. While I wasn't alone exactly, our family was alone—and that was every bit as bad. The sunbeams that had kept us company earlier transformed into sinister shadows at my feet and twisted the solitude of the trail into a lonelier place with each step I took. I wondered where the bear danger lay, what exactly it was, and what had possessed us to walk the lonely road less traveled instead of inching along the crowded, figure-eight highway that wound through the park, safe and secure in our vehicle.

What's true on the trail is true in my life: I want to take the road less traveled. I also want to feel comfortable and safe. Rarely is this the same road.

When the bridge—a naturally-occurring rhyolite arch—came into view, we paused just long enough to marvel at the topography of the landscape and the trees scratching out an existence on the surrounding rock. We didn't linger. We were ready to be away from that forest and its warning sign. Beyond that, there wasn't anything more to do besides look. Park regulations prohibit the crossing of Natural Bridge. Even stone can be crushed by the cumulative number of feet that walk this trail. After an uncomfortable and unexpected steep descent down a thin, rock-strewn path, we emerged once again into the bright, dappled light of the main trail.

We'd nearly reached the trailhead when the backcountry silence was broken by the sounds of civilization—the low hum of a motor and some unidentifiable clanking. Before long, a National Park Service truck came into view, towing something noisy behind. Stepping aside to make space for the pickup to pass, I saw the source of the sound. It was a bear trap, probably headed for the forbidden forest beyond where our trail had turned.

I sighed. Jaime and the kids seemed fine, but I was ready to get my family and myself off the trail and into our van—at least for a little while. When it came to the rigors of the road less traveled, Jaime was already comfortable. The kids were young and learning all the time. I was supposed to be all grown up, but it seemed I still had a long way to go. The wilderness was always teaching me something. While this hadn't been the most comfortable hike I'd ever taken, I knew more about taking the narrow way and facing the lonely path at the end than I did when we set out. And I knew that if I wanted my kids to be comfortable winding their way into new territory and finding the way home, I had to be willing to do the same things myself. While I was ready for a break from the trail, I wasn't done with the wilderness. And I was pretty sure it wasn't done with me.

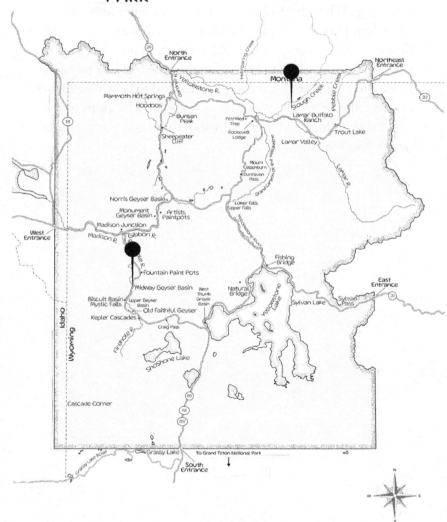

17 READING RIVERS

Halfway across the bridge at Midway, I realized I was walking alone. Looking back, I saw Jaime still on the other side, crouched down on the sidewalk studying something. This was Jaime's favorite geyser basin, home to his favorite thermal feature, the immense Excelsior Geyser Crater. I couldn't imagine what might have stopped him.

Bordered on three sides by bleached bluffs, Excelsior's shroud of steam occasionally rolls back, revealing a pool so rich and clear it calls to mind a travel poster for a tropical sea—so much so that, each time I pass by, I'm beset with a disquieting temptation to dive in. This, combined with its massive outflow cascading down the slope to the Firehole River, captured Jaime's attention from the beginning. Back in the 1880s, Excelsior erupted regularly with a magnitude befitting the size of its crater but, because things are always changing beneath the surface, it slipped into dormancy by the end of the century. One hundred years later, it roused from its slumber for two days of frequent eruptions. Not only does Jaime hope this will happen again, his wish is to drop everything, head west, and arrive in time to see it. Excelsior's blend of water, beauty, immensity, history, and mystery may well have meant love at first sight—at least for Jaime.

Standing at the end of the bridge watching him, I realized that his trained eye had seen what mine had missed: an insect hatch. Even Excelsior couldn't compete with that.

Several years earlier, Jaime and I had taken a winding path through a sparse wood of Douglas fir and yellow-tinged aspen to Slough Creek Trail's first meadow, an idyllic spot complete with a snug cabin near the banks of a meandering creek and snowcapped peaks in the distance. From the top of a rock outcropping that rose from the meadow, we basked in the afternoon sun and our proximity to mountain-clear water where a fly fisherman stood calf-deep in the creek, absorbed in his rhythmic casts. We'd seen him earlier—sprinting past us on the trail, his Teva-clad feet covered in dust and a fly rod shoved down the back of his shirt. Content on our perch in the high-country meadow, we studied him, mesmerized by the fluid ballet of fisherman, water, and line. I never saw him make a catch, but Jaime did.

A year later we were back in the park, Jaime's shiny new fly rod, flies, and gadget-gilded vest ready for their christening. Stationed on the bank of the Firehole River and surrounded by a bewildering array of fly fishing accoutrements, he clutched his copy of *Fly Fishing for the Compleat Idiot* like a life preserver. I settled in across the water, cradled in my Crazy Creek chair—a chair designed to make just sitting there, when "there" is on the ground, more comfortable. With my books, sketch pad, and paints at my side, I watched and waited. At length, Jaime stood and made his first cast. Like the man we'd seen at Slough Creek, he worked the line back and forth, searching for a cadence of his own, stopping occasionally to consult his book or extricate a fly from the tall, dry grass along the bank.

As he fished his way upstream, a small band of bison grazed their way into my field of vision. From where I sat, I could see why inexperienced park visitors often assume they are slow, docile, and disinterested. But after having to share the road with them in the winter, I had no desire to ever be so close to one again. I stood, even though they were a long way off. As the bison drifted closer, Jaime waded further upstream. I gathered my scattered belongings, and the bison advanced, looming larger with every step. Jaime, still fishing his way upstream, was on the verge of disappearing from view.

I was folding my chair when he returned from the river. Walking toward me, he pointed and said, "The bison are getting too close." They must have felt the same, because they changed course as we turned toward our vehicle.

He didn't hook one trout that day. Still, it was a beginning. Four fly fishing guides, two float trips, and unnumbered hours alone on the water later, he'd cultivated not only the ability to catch what he came for but also a deep affection for the art of fly fishing and the places trout live. Whether in sandaled feet and shorts in late summer or boots and waders in the fall, fly fishing's hold on him reaches beyond his quest to land a trout. He goes to the water for more than a catch. He's after the whistle of the line slicing through the air and the rush of water swirling around his feet and spilling over boulders. He reads rivers like I read books— his polarized eyes exploring the wilderness beneath the surface—a world as wild and varied as the one above. And when he catches his trout, he admires it, just for a moment, and gently returns it to the river.

Reading rivers has only increased Jaime's love for water of all kinds. From the beginning, a visit to Yellowstone meant a stop at Midway Geyser Basin. Now it means a stop at Midway's footbridge to study the Firehole River and the thriving insect population that makes it such a good home for trout—and their fishermen.

So on that September evening when I found myself alone on

the bridge at Midway, I knew we'd be there awhile. His gaze fixed on the river, Jaime was wholly engrossed. When I returned to him, he stood and handed me his polarized sunglasses so I could see what was happening in the water. He pulled me close, and we leaned against the sturdy upper beam of the bridge to watch mayfly after mayfly speed up from the riverbed and burst into flight after breaching the surface. Rising from the rippling river, each newly hatched insect joined the cloud of its brethren and drifted off on the sulfur-scented breeze. Only when the flow of flies slowed to a trickle did we move on to the thermal features up the hill. There, as always, Jaime lingered at Excelsior's crater long after our boardwalk companions had dispersed like newly hatched flies from the Firehole. On our way back to the car, we stopped again, searching for stragglers emerging from the river.

Because nature sometimes smiles on the persistent, Jaime had us back on the same bridge at the same time the next evening. He wasn't there for Excelsior or to learn the best fly to employ to make a catch. He was there for the aquatic wild—newly hatched insects making the dangerous journey past watchful, hungry trout —and he gave it the same attention and respect as he paid autumn's sparring elk and the backcountry's bear.

When we set off for Slough Creek, we expected nothing beyond a pleasant walk in the wilderness. But Jaime discovered fly fishing and, in that, we've received far more. We're learning to read not only rivers, but a little more of creation itself. We're learning to notice glimpses of goodness as expansive as the western sky. And we're learning to acknowledge the grace in it all, grace that shapes and sustains us.

18 LEARNING TO THROW FEATHERS

"This is where it really starts to get dicey," our guide called. "All the rocks are loose and anything you might be tempted to grab onto is either a rose or a raspberry."

Jaime and I were on a fly fishing trip—my first—and it wasn't just starting to get dicey. It had gotten dicey back at the fly shop, the moment the guide we'd hired to take us out for the day looked askance at my feet and asked, "Do you have a thicker pair of socks?"

We'd come to Yellowstone to celebrate our tenth anniversary—a couple of years after the fact. With all three kids old enough to stay at home with their grandparents, we headed west, setting aside a couple of days for Jaime to fish while I spent time at Old Faithful. We worried it might seem unromantic for a milestone celebration, but it worked for us. Jaime could immerse himself in the world of water and fish without worrying I would get bored, and I could revisit the rhythms of my old life. It was a perfect plan, right up until the moment Jaime invited me to accompany him on a guided fly fishing trip into the backcountry.

I'd had doubts about this trip from the start. I wasn't the fishing type, I was still barely the hiking type, and a backcountry fly fishing trip combined them both. I was pretty sure I wouldn't catch a single fish. Yellowstone is catch-and-release country, meaning the fish that inhabit its rivers have been caught a time or two. I figured they were smart—too smart to be tricked by someone like me. For all those reasons, I didn't want to go. But Jaime had invited me, and I didn't want to turn him down.

When we arrived at the fly shop, I was wearing tennis shoes and white crew socks. When I told our guide that, no, I did not have thicker socks, he shrugged, asked our shoe sizes, and disappeared into the back of his shop. When he returned, he handed Jaime a pair of the recommended felt-soled boots, glanced disapprovingly at my feet, and said, "These are the smallest I have. Let's see how they work."[1]

They didn't.

They were men's boots, more than two sizes too big. Jaime used all the lacing and tying tricks he knew from his hockey-playing days to shrink the space between the boot and my foot. Even so, the fit was pretty bad. When our guide told us to follow him to his rig, I clomped along behind, wishing I could be excused for the day like back in P.E. class.

Jaime and I climbed into the back seat of the ancient Blazer, and we headed into Yellowstone. Not long after we entered the park, our guide pointed at an orange Subaru situated on the shoulder near the Gardner River. "If you ever see that guy," he said, "fish somewhere else. He'll have fished it over and you won't catch anything."

This may have been the best guidance he gave Jaime all day.

Jaime sat close beside me and held my hand, perhaps in case I tried to escape. I considered my boots and wondered exactly how far into the backcountry we'd be hiking. At Mammoth Hot Springs, we turned toward the park interior, passing the Hoodoos

---

1. Felt-soled wading boots make navigating uneven, rocky, slippery waterways easier—and probably safer—when fly fishing. However, because the transfer of microscopic, non-native aquatic wildlife from one location to another is a problem in many lakes, rivers, and streams, and because it is easy for such wildlife to cling to felt, these boots are no longer allowed in many places—Yellowstone included.

then the Golden Gate area where the road had collapsed during the 1959 earthquake. Once past those, I returned my attention to my feet.

The vehicle slowed, and we turned in at a picnic area. *Why are we stopping here?* I wondered. It was a lovely place and one of our family's favorite spots to picnic, but I couldn't imagine why we were there. Then our guide hopped out of his rig and opened the tailgate. Apparently, we were there to fish.

Pointing at the concrete building behind him, he asked, "Anyone need to use the can?"

I raised my eyebrows at Jaime. I knew what the guide meant, of course, but no one, in all my thirty-four years of existence, had ever used that particular phrase with me. According to Jaime's magazines, fly fishing was gaining popularity among women. Based on boot size options and word choice, however, our guide seemed disinclined to cater to this demographic.

After grabbing our gear, Jaime and I fell in step behind him. Not far down the trail, I discovered I was in for a long trek. Jaime had made only one request: get us far enough into the backcountry that we wouldn't hear any traffic. With limited time and a long way to go, our guide set a quick pace. This would have been a noble thing, had he outfitted me with boots that fit my feet.

The trail was increasingly littered with stumps, loose rocks, and downed trees for me to haul myself and my boots over, so hiking was awkward and slow. Between those obstacles and the need to stop every few steps to shove my toes back into the front of my boots in a vain attempt to ward off blisters, it was hard to keep up and harder yet to maintain the appearance that I had ever ventured far enough off a city sidewalk to belong anywhere near the backcountry. My pride was as broken as my skin, but I was more relieved than embarrassed at the thought of a backcountry rescue.

Jaime, who'd been bolstering me with encouraging smiles ever since the sock question, looked to be in the kind of shock that leaves a man to wonder exactly how much adventure his wife can

—or perhaps will—take and if she'll be speaking to him when they return to the hotel. It was a reasonable question. In the past, I'd looked back on our hike to Slough Creek and Jaime's introduction to fly fishing as a good day. But now we were heading into the backcountry in the clutches of a recreationally unstable fishing guide on a trek that looked to be the end of me. Jaime did his best to mitigate the situation, bridging the gap between our guide and me. To his credit, he not only carried my gear, he hovered closer to my end of our little party than to our guide's.

When a solitary fly fisherman appeared on the trail behind us, our guide told us—rather indiscreetly—that he hoped the man would stop at the first hole. When he didn't, our guide grumbled —even more indiscreetly—that sometimes fishermen follow guides, tailing them to find the good spots, and that this guy must be following us. Then, ranting something about the second hole, he cut loose with a stream of expletives.

The fisherman vanished.

Even when I'm wearing well-fitting shoes that belong to me, I'm quite adept at falling over my own feet, so I watch the trail for the ever-present rocks and roots that lie in wait to trip me. The further we hiked, the less distinct the path became, eventually fading into nonexistence. At some point, I managed to catch up enough to our guide to speak to him. Hauling myself over a boulder, I said, "You must know this area well. The trail is kind of ... faint."

He laughed. "Yeah, when you get this far out, the trail gets pretty imaginary." After a long silence, he added, "I know where I'm going, though."

As he turned and moved down the trail, the weight of the fact that the man I was following into the wilderness felt the need to defend his backcountry knowledge settled on me. Until that moment it hadn't occurred to me that he might not know where he was going.

Eventually, we reached an obstacle-free meadow, and I was able to look at more than the path at my feet. A meandering river and distant mountain peaks called to mind the view from the first meadow at Slough Creek where this fly fishing business began. Just as I opened my mouth to tell Jaime as much, our guide called out—quite cheerfully—"This is where it really starts to get dicey."

Jaime and I looked at each other. We looked at our guide—or at where he should have been. The man was gone. Together, we made our way to where it seemed his voice had come from and found ourselves standing at the top of a briar-covered cliff. We peered over the edge, and there he was, sliding down a trail suitable for a mountain goat or bighorn sheep, toward the Gardner River.

"All the rocks are loose, and anything you might be tempted to grab onto is either a rose or a raspberry," he called without looking up.

Incredulous, and with a hint of accusation, I looked at Jaime. "He expects me to follow him down *that*?"

Trout dwell in beautiful places, places I've traveled to and places I've seen as I've perused Jaime's fly fishing magazines. At one time the sport had a motto: *Fly fishing: the quiet sport*. It's a motto perfectly matched to people who have romantic notions about life. And I have romantic notions about life. Notions our guide was crushing. Methodically and ruthlessly.

For Jaime, who possesses the agility of a mountain goat, our situation presented only one problem: me. He looked at me with real fear, wondering exactly what I was going to do. I was wondering that myself. It was a sunny meadow, ideal for an afternoon with a book. The day was lovely; the view, exquisite. It would have been perfect except for the fact that this meadow was exactly the type of place I believed I would be if I were a bear. Between my state of utter booklessness and my fear of meeting a bear in the backcountry, I had no choice.

"Well, we came to fish," I said, trying my best to sound happy to be part of this recreational nightmare.

Jaime dropped over the edge before I finished speaking, so

quickly I wondered if he feared I might change my mind. I sat down and scooted forward in search of a place for my feet. Gravity promptly took over. Scooting turned to sliding, which became grabbing onto the aforementioned flesh-piercing rose and raspberry canes in a desperate attempt to slow down. That I would fall was a given. That Jaime, the sure-footed one, fell first was a gift that soothed my rumpled ego.

"Will we go back the way we came?" I asked after the cliff dumped us, bruised and bleeding, at the Gardner's edge. I dreaded the answer but needed to know.

"No, we'll wade upstream and get out there," our guide answered.

Why in the world did you not bring us in that way?

Grumbling to myself about the guide's methods, I committed my feet to the clear Gardner River one timid step at a time, apprehensive about the inevitable sting on the raw skin of my heels. Once the initial smart subsided, the cold numbed my torn feet. It was September. Spring's snowmelt was done, and the summer sky was dry. The water drifted past at a leisurely pace, winding its way north toward its union with the Yellowstone River.

This is not always the Gardner's pace. One May we'd seen it swollen and angry, bolting toward the park border, inches below the footbridge where we stood with my mom and dad and our baby boy. Days later, it swept the bridge away.

The present day's gentle movement did nothing to deliver me from the difficulty of my boot situation. On land, my feet swam in my boots. In the water, they floated about, rendering the intended clinging pointless. I stood near the shore while our guide situated Jaime in his fishing spot. When it was my turn, I toddled over the dinner-plate-sized stones that lined the riverbed to the place the guide had chosen for me.

"I'm going to teach you to throw feathers," he said after stationing me on a small sandbar in the middle of the river. Then he began to school me in the art of fly fishing. I cast. And cast.

And cast again. I learned to land the fly where the trout should be, and I actually caught one—a little brown.

Jumping and cheering like a parent in the throes of potty training, our guide exclaimed, "You did it! You did it! You caught a trout! You did something that millions of people have never done, have never even thought about doing. You caught a trout. And you caught a trout in Yellowstone!"

It seemed I'd earned a spot in an elite little group. By day's end, I'd landed three trout, two browns and a rainbow. Content after accomplishing something I didn't think I could do, I spent a happy afternoon engrossed in throwing feathers to where the trout should be. Then our guide announced it was time to go.

Under the influence of the mountains in the distance and the melodic song of the river, I'd put the misery of the hike out of my mind. With no other way back, I turned my unwieldy boots and toddled to where our guide stood with Jaime. The stones were slippery, and the water swirled around my free-floating feet as I tried to find footing on the rock-lined riverbed. Every step presented an opportunity to pitch into the Gardner's chilly water.

As is his way, Jaime took my equipment. With both arms available for balance, I followed our guide as he led us upstream between the river's narrowing banks. The previously ankle-deep water rose to my calves and then my knees. Walking through the shallow places had been hard. Dragging my disembodied feet through the deepening water felt dangerous, mostly to my dignity. It must have looked dangerous, too, because our guide offered me his hand. Swallowing the shredded vestiges of my pride, I took it. A placid spot on the surface indicated an even deeper stretch ahead, so Jaime rearranged the rods and took my other hand. Hand in hand, the three of us trudged through thigh-high water, me relying on both Jaime and our guide to stay upright.

Eventually, the river widened, its water once again rippling lazily around my ankles. Our guide dropped my hand and sprinted ahead. Remembering the cliff, I wondered, *What now?*

Still holding hands—no longer from necessity but because it's our way—Jaime and I walked to where the man stood waiting for us. When we reached him, he gestured upstream and fell in step beside us. As we rounded a bend in the river, the view opened to reveal a wide, cascading waterfall, sparkling as it skimmed over a long series of low ledges in the late afternoon sun. We stopped, stunned by the diamond staircase set in the rugged Yellowstone wilderness.

"I call it Stair-Step Falls," our guide said shyly, almost as if he had made it himself. He offered it as a gift, or maybe a reward, following a difficult trip into the backcountry.

We stood together for a long time, mesmerized by the shimmering water. With the sun sinking low in the sky, we walked up the long staircase in the wilderness. At the top, I could see that the trail from the river led up to the one we'd come in on earlier. That we could have skipped the bruising, flesh-tearing cliff was as clear as the Gardner itself.

Why in the world didn't he bring us in this way? I wondered again.

Still grumbling, I turned for a final look at the waterfall and saw the answer to my question. The molten silver staircase resulted from the angle of the afternoon sun. It wouldn't have been so lovely in the morning, and it wouldn't have meant as much at the beginning of the day as it did at the end. That was why he didn't bring us in this way. His choice of path wasn't random or thoughtless. It was purposeful.

Our guide did, indeed, know where he was going.

Above the song of the river, I picked up a soft refrain: *Well done, good and faithful servant.* It wasn't a declaration of what was but a whisper of what could be—the reward at the end of a life of following well. It wasn't an announcement of arrival but an invitation to learn to walk with a guide.

Walking with a guide has a great deal to do with trust, and I was no better at it in the terrain of my everyday life than out here in the wilderness. Dissatisfaction with my equipment, disdain for the trail, and fear about cliffs of all kinds—none of this was new territory. Just as in the backcountry, I'm prone to grumble over every inconvenient, painful, scary, and humbling thing that comes my way. Whether transitory irritations or persistent trials, it's easy for me to ignore that these things serve an important purpose: they get me from where I am to where I want to be and help me grow along the way. Dicey or not, this is exactly what the trail our guide chose accomplished.

Following is an act of faith—one that sometimes means managing ill-fitting equipment, traveling through tough terrain, or clinging to my guide's hand as I pass through pools too deep to navigate on my own. But this is how we get there—to the final destination and every stop in between. Left to myself, I would never have taken that trail. I wouldn't have risked the blisters or braved the cliff. I wouldn't have caught the trout. And I would have missed the waterfall that showed me a little something about navigating life. But I wasn't left to myself. I had a guide. And I didn't miss a thing.

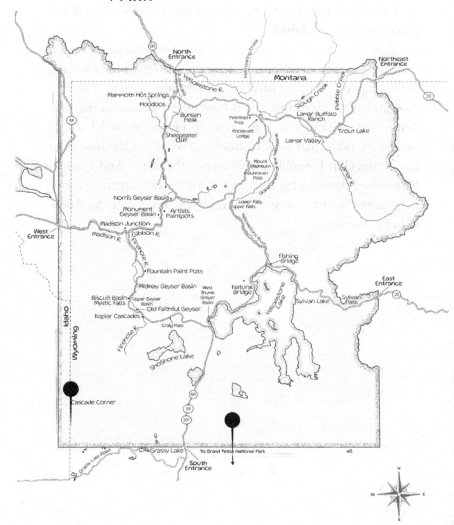

19 DON'T WORRY

Once in a while, even though we didn't see ourselves as camping sorts, Jaime and I detoured through one of Yellowstone's small campgrounds. We enjoyed searching for the perfect campsite—one hidden among the trees, preferably near the water. As we passed tents with cars, vans, and SUVs parked next to them, I envisioned house-locking, car-alarm installing, security system-owning city folk getting back to nature by sleeping under fabric. *Fabric.* I've never been able to reconcile that in my mind.

Camping, with its ambiance of evening fires and constant proximity to trees and fresh air, fits my romantic notions about life. I like the idea of camping. It's the reality of the hard ground, unpredictable weather, and lack of shower facilities I find distressing. During our visits to the campgrounds, though, I started noticing tentless people surrounded by their bikes and backpacks, cooking over fires and enjoying the outdoors before climbing into their vans and SUVs, locking up, and falling asleep on a stack of memory foam with no concern about weather, wildlife, or criminals.

That looked interesting—so interesting that, in 2008, Jaime

and I decided to join them. And, because one new experience wasn't enough, we added a second. We brought our canoe along.

We left the kids safe at home with Mom and Dad and set off, ready to conquer the wilderness, our red Mad River canoe cresting the top of our van like the plume on a Roman soldier's helmet. We hadn't gone far before Jaime noticed the canoe wasn't sitting square. At the next exit, he slowed down, pulled off, and adjusted it. Within a few miles, the straps were slapping the windshield so we stopped again. And again. Instead of marching down I-80 like a battle-ready Roman soldier, we were limping along like one of the conquered.

"We need some different straps," Jaime said. "There's a new Cabela's in Omaha. We can stop there." We parked at the back of the lot and, in the fastest Cabela's stop in the history of our marriage, made our purchase and returned to the van.

"We'll take it off on the driver's side," Jaime said as he began loosening the straps.

I stared at him. "Um ... I've never lifted the canoe."

He and Mason always loaded and unloaded it back home. Somehow I'd managed to overlook the fact that, if the canoe was going to do more than go along for the ride, I was going to have to figure out how to help maneuver it.

"You can do it. You're stronger and more stable since your knee surgery. You take the front." He waited while I moved to the front of the van. "We'll lift on three. One. Two. Three."

We lifted it up, moved it over, and lowered it to the ground.

Jaime smiled. "See? I knew you could do it." It took him only a few seconds to position the canoe pads.

"Okay! Let's put it back. Just grab onto each side at the front and lift. On three again."

We lifted. The canoe came off the ground easily, at least it was easy until my legs and back were straight and I had to use my arms. I bobbled and lifted and bobbled some more while Jaime muscled it up and onto the van. That done, he cinched it down with the new straps, and we drove away.

After our backcountry fly fishing trip, we'd decided I am not a fisherman. So I dropped Jaime off in Riverton, Wyoming, to fish with his brother's mountain-residing brother-in-law while I spent a sunny late-summer day drifting through the shopping district in nearby Lander. Leaving myself just enough time to return to Riverton to purchase the week's groceries and meet Jaime, I forced myself from the local indie bookstore, reached into my purse for my keys, and found nothing.

I stopped and looked.

Nothing.

With a familiar knot gripping my stomach, I sat down on a bench and searched the recesses of my purse.

Still nothing.

I knew where they were—on the driver's seat next to my phone, both tossed absentmindedly aside and left behind in their new habitual home, the spot that made our Triple A membership a better deal for us than for them. After walking to the van and confirming the location of the keys, I crossed the road to the payphone, made the call, and sat down on a bench to wait. According to the sign on the bank, it was one hundred degrees, a reality that hadn't registered as I'd strolled from one air-conditioned boutique to another under the wide awnings of the main street. After an hour and a half of sweltering in the late afternoon sun and seeing exactly no vehicles, a dusty blue pickup sputtered into town and parked behind my van. Its wiry driver shuffled toward me, situated his box on the concrete, and withdrew the tools of his trade—tools far different than the shiny metal hooks used by the teenager who regularly rescued me back home. With worn wooden wedges, he freed me in less time than it had taken him to unfold himself from his antiquated truck.

I'd barely passed Lander's city limits when my phone rang.

"Hey, Babe," Jaime said, sounding cheerful after his day outdoors.

"Hey. How was fishing?"

"It was great. We spent the day about an hour outside

Riverton. I caught a half dozen—all good-sized browns. How about you? Did you have a good day?"

"Yeah. I had a nice day." I sighed. "And then when it was time to leave to buy groceries I couldn't find my keys and had to call Triple A."

"Are you okay? Where are you?"

"I'm okay ... but it took the locksmith forever to get to Lander, so I'm barely out of town and I don't have the groceries and we're going to be late," I said, fighting back tears.

"Late where?" Jaime asked gently. "We can get the groceries together and we don't have anything we have to do besides find a campground. Don't worry. It will all be okay."

The sun was slipping from the sky by the time we left the grocery store. We'd decided to risk not having a reservation that night because we weren't sure when Jaime would finish fishing and we figured we could find something along the way. Back home it had seemed adventurous. On the twilight road to the Tetons, it seemed foolish.

The sun dropped, and darkness descended in the sudden way of the mountain sky. While county, state, and some national park campgrounds are large affairs with loops of sites backed up into rows of trees, national forest campgrounds are intimate to the point of isolation. By day I find this charming. By night I would rather be in a hotel, safe behind a locked door. Because of the key fiasco, it was night before we even began to look. We stopped at the first campground we came to.

It was full.

We pulled into the next one.

It, too, was full.

I eyed the mom-and-pop hotels we passed as we traveled along and wondered exactly how bad a miscalculation we'd made. Jaime's fishing partner had told him there was a nice parking lot right off the highway at a lake along the way that we could sleep at if we got desperate. Earlier it had seemed like a kind thing to say.

Now it sounded like local-ese for *What were you thinking? It's Saturday night in the mountains. The campgrounds will be full.*
   I knew that lake. It was lovely. I just didn't want to sleep in a parking lot between the highway and the public bathroom. Still, I wondered if it was our only hope as we passed by.
   We pulled into another campground, and I could tell by the cadence of Jaime's footsteps when he ran back to the car that he'd secured a spot. Moments later, gravel crunched under our tires as he drove up the hill to our solitary site. While Jaime backed into place, I surveyed our surroundings by headlight as they sliced through the night. It was a cozy little campsite, set back among the pines. I'm sure I would have loved it if we'd arrived in the afternoon. But it was nine o'clock at night. We'd planned to cook dinner, but it was pitch black. And we were on a dead end at the top of a hill, alone in a Brothers Grimm-esque forest. I felt the presence of some legendary grizzly lurking behind a tree—paws poised and colossal claws extended—ready to reach out, drag me deeper into the woods, and devour me as soon as I stepped out of the van. If he didn't get me, I knew the deranged ax-murderer who had surely escaped from the nearest penitentiary that day and was obviously making his way to the Tetons through this forest, would.
   "It's kind of dark and creepy out there," I said. "I don't really want to get out."
   "We could forget dinner and just head to bed," Jaime offered.
   Without fire or food, we climbed into the back of the van and settled our sunburned bodies into our double sleeping bag on its memory foam base. Jaime knew all about the bears and killers running wild and free in my head. In the seconds it took him to sink into a deep sleep, he pulled me close, close enough to feel safe as I contemplated the lonely silence of the wilderness.
   The morning sun appeared as quickly as it had vanished the night before, brightening the sky and illuminating a sweet mountain campsite tucked away in the trees. The legendary bear and the

escaped prisoner both evaporated in the light of the new day. There was nothing here to fear. This campsite was perfect. Still, I hoped the next occupants would be fortunate enough to find it before dark.

20 THAT WASN'T IN THE FORECAST

"There they are."

Jaime decelerated. He'd been watching for this since we'd driven away from the campground—waiting for the tunnel of trees we'd been traveling through to open up and reveal the granite faces of the Tetons. Smitten with this view since he first saw it in deep winter a few years back, he stopped at every turnout we came to—sometimes for a photo, other times simply to stand in the crisp morning air and absorb the scene. The mountains of Grand Teton National Park, especially the three that anchor the range, are the mountains children draw—tall triangles, sharp peaks topped with snow. This is the Cathedral Group, made up of Teewinot Mountain, the Grand Teton, and Mount Owen.

The two main roads in Grand Teton National Park don't lead into the mountains. They pass in front of them. At Moran Junction, we turned toward Oxbow Bend, a tranquil arc in the Snake River, and at Jenny Lake Junction, we turned toward the visitor center to check the weather report. The sky was clear and, according to the posting, so was the forecast. Clear weather confirmed, we launched our canoe.

Every time we pass by the Tetons we stop at String Lake, and almost every time we stop we picnic at one of the two tables along the shore. Whether we picnic or not, Jaime and the kids always skip a few rocks or launch a beached log back into this long strip of water at the foot of Mount Moran.

Elyse's first memory—not just of the mountains but of her life—is from String Lake. We were heading home after spending a week in Yellowstone with Mom and Dad, and stopped there for one last picnic lunch. Then fifteen months old, Elyse finished eating long before the rest of us, so we let her toddle around. Her explorations led her to an unused fire ring.

"You know she's playing by a fire ring, don't you?" Dad asked.

"Yeah," Jaime said. "I'm keeping an eye on her."

Jaime and I have never been the type of parents who worry a lot about keeping our children and their clothes clean when they play outside. In an era of washing machines and hot running water, laundry and baths aren't that difficult to deal with. But by the time we finished lunch, Elyse looked like a street urchin from a Dickens novel. Even Jaime and I couldn't just put her in the car. She needed a bath. We had running water, in the form of a spigot that gushed glacial-cold liquid, and we had heat, in the form of a camp stove. So we warmed the water and put it, along with Elyse, in our dishpan and bathed her. Incensed, her howls spread through the stillness of the otherwise vacant picnic area and rose over our heads to the treetops and toward the jagged peak of Mount Moran. While Elyse remembers the indignity of her outdoor bath, it's the adults who remember the details.

Usually, these stops are more peaceful. More often than not, a pair of kayakers will paddle past, and we'll watch from the shore in reverent silence as their bows slice through the still water. String Lake and its kayakers were the reason we brought the canoe to the Tetons, but at less than a mile and a half long and much less than half a mile wide, it's primarily a throughway for paddlers traveling to Leigh Lake.

When it came time to launch, Jaime and I settled the canoe on the still, icy water, walked it out to knee height, and climbed in. Jaime, because he knows how to steer, sat in the back of the canoe and I, because I do not, sat in front. And just like that, we were in the moment that brought us to this place.

String Lake's crystal water simultaneously revealed the view below and reflected the one above. Occasional boulders broke through cotton candy clouds and craggy peaks shimmering on the surface. Paddling past them, we paused occasionally to examine the mosaic of small, smooth stones that lined the lake. It was a quick trip to the far shore, where we joined a surprising bottleneck of paddlers preparing to portage to the larger lake beyond.

Jaime hopped out of the canoe and held it steady while I searched for solid footing on the pebbled lakebed. We pulled it to shore and joined the band of pilgrims portaging their vessels to Leigh Lake. Turns out, taking the canoe off the van and putting it back on was nothing in comparison to carting our craft from one place to another. I'd always thought of it as our little red canoe which, given that it could safely and comfortably hold our family of five, was ridiculous. In truth, it was a beast. While it was smooth on the water, it was awkward and hulking on land. Once again, if it was going to go anywhere, I was going to have to help move it. We picked it up, Jaime carrying the front and me wobbling along behind, making our way over a path overrun with boulders of various sizes to the narrow chute that served as the backcountry boat launch.

Leigh Lake dwarfed String Lake. Still, it was a cozy place, enveloped, as it was, by pines. We made our way down the western shore, our canoe slicing through the reflection of Mount Moran's jagged peak. Craning our necks over the side of the canoe, we glided past the bungalow-sized boulders below the glassy surface.

Two-thirds of the way down the shore, we found ourselves across from an island, so we ventured across open water to paddle around it. It wasn't long before the smooth veneer that beckoned us to the island lost its sheen, and we broke for the opposite bank over rapidly developing rollers. We'd read about this—about being careful not to get caught in the middle of the lake by afternoon thunderstorms. But in the face of a clear forecast and calm water, we'd forgotten. When we reached the far shore, the sun was still shining. Backpackers were still making their way toward their backcountry campsites. Kayakers and canoeists were still paddling around the lake. And, against swirling, gray water that no longer revealed the mosaic below nor reflected the sky above, so were we.

Thankful we were away from the island and close to shore, I checked the buckles on my life jacket. We worked our way up the shore toward the distant chute where we had put in, and I hoped the ominous sky would turn and go. Along the way, we passed a trio who had pulled their canoe up the beach and sat, tucked in to watch the approaching storm. Fighting increasingly large whitecaps, we rowed toward a point upshore. As we rounded it, the storm declared its intentions with a wintery wind that whipped down from the mountain and manhandled our boat. We'd never encountered water like that. Uncertain of what to do, I whirled around to ask Jaime, a move that turned us parallel to the frothing waves that threatened to broadside us and swamp our boat. Shouting over the now-roaring wind, he told me how to paddle through. We managed to reach a place where we could pull our canoe out and, like the trio we had just passed, wait out the storm.

Only I was wet. And cold. And a fair-weather outdoorswoman whose expectations are admittedly not always realistic or even reasonable. I like my mountain weather sunny and seventy, with crisp mornings and cool evenings. Rain, according to my idealistic way of thinking, was simply unnecessary during the daylight hours.

"Do you think we could beach the canoe over by the trees, hike out, and come back for it in the morning?" I asked Jaime, cautious because even though I wasn't very good at it, canoeing was my thing, and adventure was his. Ditching the canoe because of a little rain was not particularly adventurous.

He looked at the stony sky and churning lake, and then he

looked at me. "That'll work," he said after a moment's consideration.

We dragged our canoe to the trees, found the trail, and hiked out against wind and pelting rain. By the time we reached our campsite, the storm had calmed to a gentle drizzle. We prepared our evening meal at a picnic table under the sheltering pines and enjoyed what we had missed the previous night: dinner al fresco. When the rain picked up, we drove to Colter Bay's outpost of civilization. With piles of quarters for the coin-operated showers, we warmed up under hot water and walked to the gift shop to spend some time and maybe some money. Eventually, the rain became a storm. Lightning tore through the sky and knocked out the power, so we drove back to our campsite, tucked ourselves into bed, read by the light of our headlamps, and fell asleep to the rhythm of rain that hadn't stopped since we abandoned our canoe that afternoon.

Early the next morning we woke from a good night's sleep to an eerie glow. The sun was bright but unable to penetrate the snow that had piled up on our van in the night. *That* hadn't been in the forecast.

We hiked back to our canoe through an early September wonderland. Like the pines that lined the trail, it sat undisturbed under four inches of powdery snow. No longer was the shore bordered with late summer evergreen. Deep winter's heavy-laden boughs reflected off the water, the lacy trees a lovely foil against the day's flat sky. Jaime waded in first, holding the canoe steady as I rolled up my pant legs, removed my hiking sandals and socks, and stepped into the lake. The water was no colder than it had been the previous day, but wet feet don't dry quickly in the chilly air, and I shivered as our canoe sliced through the surface as we paddled along the shore toward our heated van and the mugs of hot chocolate we planned to make on our Coleman stove.

It didn't take long to warm up, so we put in again at Oxbow Bend, a popular spot for tourists hoping to see moose or otter and photographers seeking a good shot of the most photographed scene in the Tetons: Mount Moran across the water. Jaime steered away from the crowd on the river bank so we could float in the solitude of the shadow of the mountain. After our Leigh Lake adventure, we relished the slower pace of the Oxbow. Jaime watched for trout while I studied the mountain and sky beyond.

It was a short stop. We had more we wanted to do, so when our time was up, we pulled ourselves away from the river, hoisted the canoe onto the van for the final time, and headed north.

21 HIKING IN

"Do you want to hike down the Terraced Falls Trail?" Jaime asked as he drove toward the main road.

"Can we make it that far?" I replied.

"No, but we can hike a little ways. We can see a little more of this part of the park. We won't get far. Sunset's in an hour and we need to be off the trail by dark."

We'd already spent most of the day in Yellowstone's Bechler region, a less-visited, remote area of the park. Bechler, also known as Cascade Corner, was a new destination for us. It required passage over Grassy Lake Road, a one-lane, marginally maintained, dirt affair located north of the Tetons and south of Yellowstone's South Entrance. We drove almost all of its thirty-six miles to the easily accessible Cave Falls—accessible meaning that, unlike other waterfalls in the area, reaching it would not require an overnight stay in the backcountry. A three-mile hike from the parking lot took us to an overlook above Cave Falls and a short path to the cave for which it is named. While the cave is nice, it's the two-hundred-fifty-foot-wide curl of the Falls River that gives it impact.

The day was almost done when we decided to hike just a little of the Terraced Falls Trail. Jaime turned in at a small parking lot right as the sky delivered the second early September snow in two days. Few traces remained of the first, but by the time we procured our winter gear, wet heavy flakes blanketed our heads and shoulders. We entered the woods and walked several yards before arriving at the official trailhead, a small brown billboard plastered with a variety of signs—the first of which I'd never seen on a trail:

ENTERING YELLOWSTONE NATIONAL PARK

Jaime and I, it seemed, were hiking into the park from the outside, something that made me feel like I'd achieved a new level on the outdoor adventure scale. There were other notices, too, each stirring a decidedly less happy response as they silently screamed at me to not forget to be afraid:

DO NOT HIKE AFTER DARK
HIKE IN GROUPS
HIKE IN GROUPS OF 3 OR MORE

We already planned to be off the trail by dark. We knew it was best to hike in a group. And we were well aware it was best to hike in groups of three or more. That, unfortunately, is a difficult thing for a couple to pull off.

We set off down the trail, probably more quietly than we should have. It's easy to slip into silence when you walk in the wilderness. Trails are narrow, often requiring a single-file arrangement that makes conversation awkward. Because they are littered with trip hazards—loose gravel, roots, and rocks—I tend to fixate on the ground in front of me, which is to say that I focus on not falling. Concentration leads to silence. Sometimes on the trail, we have to work at talking, at making noise to make our presence known.

"We'd better turn back," Jaime said after we'd been walking for about thirty minutes.

Night falls quickly in the mountains. With no distant horizon, the sun disappears when it sinks behind the surrounding peaks, making for a quick twilight. Disquieted by the descending darkness, we opted to sing rather than converse—anything to let the bears that inhabited this less-traveled area of the park know they were not alone. While the snow had stopped long before, traces frosted the trees and the edge of the trail, a trail I watched with even more care because of the late afternoon shadows.

"What's that?" I pointed at something in the middle of the trail ahead.

Jaime looked it over. "It looks like bear scat."

I knew that. I was just hoping for a different answer. "It wasn't there when we walked in. I would have seen it. You know how I watch the ground."

"I know," he said. "Just keep moving. The trailhead is up that hill, and the van isn't far beyond."

As close as we were, we seemed to make little progress. With every step, I felt the steamy breath of a Kodiak-sized grizzly on my neck, close enough for him to reach out a silent paw and snag one of us with his claws.

When we reached the trailhead, I hiked out of Yellowstone even more happily than I had hiked in. Looking out the window from the safety of the van's fiberglass shell and automatically locking doors, it didn't seem as dark as it had in the woods.

In the morning, we drove into Yellowstone, where Jaime pulled in at a turnout a few miles past the entrance. A slim opening between the pines invited us to step away from the asphalt and into the woods. A narrow dirt path, the center aisle of a wilderness cathedral, led to a waterfall—the surrounding lodgepole pines supporting the soaring ceiling and scattering the light like so many stained-glass windows. The towering forest not only buttressed the sky, it buffered the sound of passing traffic. I sat on a log and sank into the silence while Jaime walked to the brink of the waterfall. Before long he headed back, his hands shoved deep into his pockets against the chilly morning.

"We're here," he said.

"I know. It feels different than the Tetons. We've been in the mountains for days—fly fishing, hiking, camping, canoeing ... doing things we already love or wanted to try. We've been close by, but now that we're here it just ... I don't know, it feels different."

Jaime sat down on the log and put his arms around me. "That's because we're home," he whispered.

He was right. The frontier of our life is built on the straight edges of the manmade world with its buildings and schedules, its lines to stay inside and molds to fill. Here, in the spacious light of a wilderness masterpiece shaped by a more gracious hand, we were at home. And for now, I was at peace.

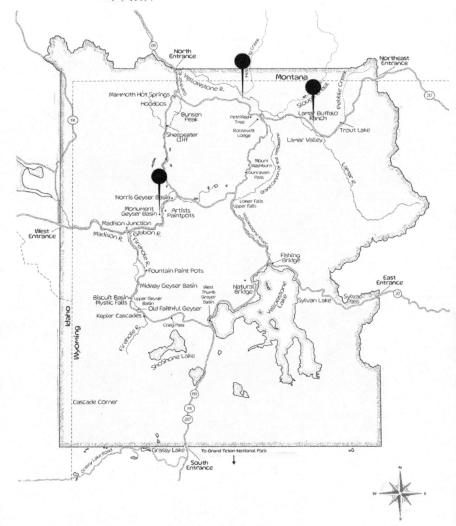

22   LAMAR BUFFALO RANCH

Three quick taps broke the stillness of our Mammoth Hot Springs Hotel room.

"Yes?" I mumbled into the dark.

"This is your wake-up knock," a chipper male voice answered from the hall.

We'd asked for this.

"Thanks," I replied. The early morning knock was Yellowstone's dignified answer to the modern wake-up call for their historic, telephone-less rooms. Jaime hadn't stirred.

"Hey, Babe," I whispered, "it's time to get up. Wolves, remember?"

Jaime threw his arm across his face.

Four in the morning was early even for me. We'd heard dawn and dusk were the best times to see wolves, however, so we dragged ourselves from our cozy bed and out into the chill of the September mountain morning. Before long, we were traveling through Yellowstone's northern range, over a section of road I used to think of as the loneliest in the park. That was before the wolves. Now its turnouts were often crowded with people, many with spotting scopes poised and binoculars at the ready. Wolves aside, at this hour the road was deserted, and I longed to be back at the hotel—asleep in our snug bed, waking only when morning's gentle light warmed our window. Jaime slowed the van and eased into a small, semi-circular turnout.

"What are we doing?" I asked, vacillating between worry that something was wrong with the vehicle and suspicion that Jaime was stopping for the sole purpose of checking something out, something he would want to share with me.

"Pulling over so we can get out and look at the sky," Jaime answered.

I groaned inwardly. Forever curious, Jaime was exploring. In the middle of the night. On a dark and deserted road. In the wilderness. He opened his door, an invitation for the night air to brush my face with its icy fingers.

"It's cold," I protested. "And dark."

"It'll be okay. Wait there. I'll come around for you."

He opened my door and found my hand. With one in his and the other on the van, I took one sightless step after another as he led me around the back of the vehicle. He stationed himself against the driver's side and I settled against him—both to reassure myself that he was there and to absorb some warmth from his body.

"Close your eyes," Jaime said.

Really? I couldn't believe he would evict me from the comfort of our warm van out into the cold night just to kiss me. Except that I could. Even with all my fanciful notions, Jaime's the romantic and I am, well, less so. I closed my eyes and waited.

"What?" I asked finally, wondering why I was standing on the side of the road in the heaviest part of the night with my eyes shut.

"It's as black with your eyes open as with them closed. It's that dark," Jaime said, comfortable both with our surroundings and his conviction that stopping to contemplate the depth of the darkness was worth a few minutes of discomfort.

I opened my eyes. It *was* that dark. Unlike Jaime, I was neither comfortable with our surroundings nor convinced this momentary misery was worth it. I shivered, and he wrapped his arms around me, a shield against the intensity of the night.

From there, the road wound upward from Mammoth Hot Springs, past the turnouts to Petrified Tree and Blacktail Plateau Drive. We navigated more by memory than by landmark as we made our way through our headlight tunnel. Only when we arrived at Tower Junction, near the western-themed Roosevelt Lodge dating back to the 1920s, could we see exactly where we were. The northern part of the park reveals the vastness of Yellowstone's landscape and its expansive sky. Lodgepole pines that frame the road nearly everywhere else are absent here, replaced by open terrain dotted with Douglas fir, aspen, and sage. This is the Lamar Valley, known as the American Serengeti for the large numbers of large mammals—wolves, bears, bison, and elk among them—spread across the sweeping landscape.

Today, park policy is to let life in the wild unfold and run its course as its rivers do—naturally, without interference. This has not always been so. During the early years, Yellowstone's stewards seemed to divide the park's animals into two types: desirable and undesirable. Predatory animals such as coyotes, mountain lions, and wolves ate desirable animals such as deer and elk. This cast the predators in an undesirable light, and they were hunted to near or complete eradication in the park. When the hunting down was done and wildlife management practices changed, the resilient coyote population rebounded on its own. Mountain lions followed the same path, although at a much slower pace. Wolves did not. For them to be part of the Yellowstone ecosystem once again would require help, help that came in the form of reintroduction.

Part of that work took place in the Lamar Valley—specifically at the Lamar Buffalo Ranch. Named for its location and original mission, it's an anomaly among the park's settlements. With no gas stations, stores, hotels, or restaurants, it has none of the crowd and hubbub of the other developed areas. Even the official use of the word *buffalo* in the ranch's name is unusual. While visitors often use the word *buffalo*, park literature and employees use the word *bison*. While both are technically correct, *bison* is more formal and favored in the scientific community. Perhaps the people who named the Lamar Buffalo Ranch were informal, non-scientific sorts who just wanted to do their job, which was to build the herd.

Back in the 1800s, buffalo were said to number in the tens of millions across North America—an amount impossible for me to imagine. By the beginning of the 1900s, the population had dwindled to only a few hundred, twenty-five of them residing in Yellowstone. To restore and rebuild the park's wild herd, the National Park Service brought a similar number of domesticated bison to the park. For four decades they corralled and cared for them in the Lamar Valley. Over time, they were released into the park to breed with Yellowstone's wild bison. By the early 1950s, the herd had grown to a sustainable size, and the work of ranching came to an end.

Building the bison herd wasn't the only restoration work carried out at the Lamar Buffalo Ranch. In the 1990s, after seventy years of stewarding Yellowstone and learning how to manage the park and its resources, the National Park Service obtained permission to make another course correction. They set about reversing the eradication of one of the park's predatory animals and brought the ranch back into service for another unusual assignment: the reintroduction of Yellowstone's wolves.

In January of 1995, the winter before Jaime and I took our first trip to the park together, fourteen gray wolves arrived in Yellowstone. They'd been caught in Canada, collared for tracking purposes, and conveyed to the park. I watched the news coverage from home as, with a degree of fanfare, they were transported through the Roosevelt Arch past spectators who'd come to celebrate, or at least bear witness to, something historic. Upon arrival, they were taken to remote areas and placed in acclimation pens of approximately an acre in size, an area large enough to contain a social group—or what we might think of as a pack. One of these pens was near the Lamar Buffalo Ranch.

Park employees observed the wolves from a distance and delivered food with as little interaction as possible, hoping to increase the likelihood that the wolves would adjust to their new surroundings and make Yellowstone their home. After ten weeks, close to spring on the calendar but still deep winter in the mountains, the pens were opened. The wolves were free. They could make their way back to Canada, or they could stay.

They stayed.

They stayed, and their presence gave rise to a new breed of Yellowstone visitor: the wolf watchers, people who gather along the road through the Lamar Valley, clustering around spotting scopes and watching for wolves. They know all about the wolves —their identification numbers, their packs, their stories. These were the people we were looking for on that dark, cold, September morning.

"Just show up," we'd been told. "Someone will tell you what's going on. If there's anything to see, someone will let you look through their scope. The wolf watchers love to show off the wolves."

We'd been told to get out there early, hence the 4 a.m. wake-up knock and subsequent drive through the dark. After passing several empty turnouts and parking areas along the road in the Lamar Valley, we realized that perhaps we'd taken the advice a little too literally. Every single one was empty. A faint glow hinted at sunrise as Jaime pulled into one and parked.

As we sat and waited for morning light to break over the landscape, a small SUV pulled in beside us. Its lone occupant climbed out, situated a pack on his back, crossed the road, and disappeared over the hill. His equipment, a handheld antenna for picking up transmissions from radio collars on park wildlife, made it obvious: he was there for the wolves. Disappointed, I watched him go. We could approach a park official standing near the turnout, but we weren't about to stalk one across the road and over the hill.

Soon, more headlights heralded a succession of cars, trucks, and SUVs full of other early risers. They pulled into our turnout, climbed out of their vehicles, set up spotting scopes, and stood—coffee in hand—waiting. These appeared to be the people we'd been told to look for—the wolves' ardent public, dedicated folk who donated time and money and declared their devotion with vanity plates bearing the number of a favored wolf. They'd put in hours armed with scopes, alert for a lingering—or maybe even a fleeting—glimpse of a wolf or a pack or a hunt. We watched and listened to them talk among themselves as they scanned the brightening horizon. Once in a while, someone would think they saw something, and Jaime would look, but our binoculars were a poor substitute for a spotting scope. That morning's wolf watchers seemed disinclined to share anything they knew about the local pack.

I'd imagined this unfolding differently. I'd expected something more from the people and probably from the wolves. I'd believed it would be easy. And predictable. Like Old Faithful. After a while, the wolf watchers decided to cross the road, and we decided to move on to other things. As I watched them climb and disappear over the same hill as the antenna-carrying man, I wondered if we would ever see a Yellowstone wolf.

23 WORTH THE WAIT

Later that day, we were back in the Lamar Valley, this time taking the sage-lined road in the early afternoon light. After a sightseeing drive to the Northeast Entrance and a short-but-strenuous hike to Trout Lake, our next destination was the suspension bridge on the Hellroaring Trail. As we wound through the undulating hills of the wide valley, we rounded a corner and saw vehicles haphazardly abandoned on both sides of the road. Jaime took his foot off the accelerator.

"What kind of jam do you think this is?" I asked. "Do you see anything?"

The elk were in rut, so it could have been one of the ever-growing harems the bulls wrangled over. It could have been a bison. They were plentiful in this part of the park.

"There are a lot of cars. It might be a bear," Jaime answered, braking lightly. "Or a wolf."

I scanned the surrounding slopes while he found an opening and maneuvered our van into place. We got out and walked a quarter-mile down the road toward a congregation of people.

"Look! Over there." He pointed down to the Lamar River, where it flowed past us on its journey toward its union with the Yellowstone. "There's an elk."

There, midstream, stood a lone female elk, wild eyes agitated and body stiff. Something wasn't right. I'd never seen an elk just standing in a river. Nor had I ever seen one so still.

"She's injured," Jaime said. "See? Look at her haunches. She has a big wound on her back leg, and I think she's got one on her side."

Then, as he's prone to do, he silently pointed at something. I looked across the water. There, on the far bank, was a wolf. Sitting beside the river, in the middle of the day, close enough for us to see without the aid of a spotting scope or even binoculars.

It was perfect. And worth the wait.

We smiled at each other and moved a little closer to get a better look. The wolf watched the elk. The elk watched the wolf. Neither seemed particularly concerned about the herd of people watching them.

We hadn't been there long before I began to wonder how long we would stay. Even on vacation, I'm always aware of the time, of how the sun marches more quickly across the sky than we progress along the trail or through our list of what we hope to do. A September afternoon in the mountains is a short-lived commodity. We needed to move on if we were going to get on the trail in time to be off before dark.

"We probably need to go soon, if we want to make the Hellroaring Trail," I said. "Unless you want to stay."

"Let's stay," Jaime said. "We can take that hike tomorrow."

He took my hand, and we walked up a steep hill on the other side of the road. We settled in an open spot among a smaller gathering of people on the slope and watched. Even from across the road, we were still close enough to see both the wolf and the elk without binoculars.

As we sat down, a man farther up the hillside filled us in. "That's the alpha female. She does all the hunting. Alone."

"Yeah," someone else called out. "The alpha male and the other males don't hunt. They let her do it. They stay home with the pups. It's a strange deal."

From various spots on the slope, the information kept coming.

"She's a good hunter. She feeds them all."

"And with a bad hip."

"She has a bad hip?" I asked.

"Yeah! She hurt it during a hunt. It still doesn't work quite right, but that doesn't stop her from bringing down big animals by herself."

The pride this little community felt for the wolf down by the river was palpable.

A man walked over to us. "You folks wanna take a look through my scope?"

Nodding, I smiled and stood. Jaime let me look first. Before I got myself square with the eyepiece someone called to him, "Here, you can look through mine."

These were the wolf watchers we'd been told about. The ones we'd been looking for that morning, the ones who were known for sharing what they knew and what they saw. Still, it was even better than I had expected and well beyond what I had imagined.

Through the scope, I noticed not only the dark gray mingled with the buff of the wolf's coat, I saw the gash in the elk's flank. Before long, the elk took a timid step forward. The wolf stood and took three strides in her direction. The elk froze. The wolf turned, walked twenty yards downstream, and went to work on a carcass she had waiting on the riverbank. When the wolf was deep into her dinner, the elk tried to slink away again, managing only a few steps before her captor covered the distance between the meal she'd been consuming and the one she had in reserve. Running through the river and stepping into the elk's path, she stopped with just inches between their noses. Again, the elk froze. Satisfied, the wolf left the water and ambled up the slope, her limp obvious as she climbed the bank. She stretched out in the sage, and even though we'd all seen where she'd settled down, even though we searched with our binoculars and spotting scopes, no one on the hill could find her. If we'd been driving past, we never would have known she was there.

Jaime and I spent a good part of the afternoon watching the wolf and the elk, and while we could have stayed longer, we were ready to move on. We weren't wolf watchers. We were generalists who had come to Yellowstone to do a little of a lot of different things. We got to spend time in company not only with a wolf, but also her prey and a group of people who'd made a hobby of watching her and her pack, and we were grateful. Besides, we both knew how it was going to end, and neither of us felt the need to stay and watch. Descending the slope, Jaime stopped occasionally to wait because his confident downhill stride outstripped my cautious, choosy steps. At the road, he took my hand and we walked to the van, got in, and drove away, leaving the elk in the river and the wolf in the sage.

Not far down the road we passed a small band of bison and a slow-moving herd of cars, their passengers craning for a better look or a good photo. Exasperated, I complained to myself. *It's not a bear or a wolf. It's just a bison. There are thousands of them in the park. You'll probably drive past a hundred of them today. Pull off the road or drive!*

And then I remembered.

Today.

There are thousands of bison today. I forget that this was not always so, that it took hard work and long years to restore Yellowstone's herd to its abundant state. Because there are so many of them, I take bison for granted.

The Lamar Buffalo Ranch, with its simple corral and its collage of buildings, some scavenged from locations throughout the park, is a humble place. Its tiny, unassuming brown sign doesn't proclaim its contributions or announce its standing on the National Register of Historic Places. Nothing about it hints that this is where people twice took on the arduous, uncertain tasks of rebuilding and restoring. What we're willing to undo is as important as what we do, and I'm grateful for quiet places like the

Lamar Buffalo Ranch that make space for the inevitable undoing of the past for the sake of the future. I'm glad for wolves, for bison, and second chances, and I'm indebted to the redeeming nature of space and grace.

I'd be lost without them.

24 BEAR FREQUENTING AREA

When Jaime and I headed to Hellroaring Creek the next morning—our packs loaded down with food, water, books, and fishing gear—we paused at the trailhead and stared at the familiar sign:

> WARNING
> BEAR
> FREQUENTING AREA

Every time I see this sign I'm as frustrated as the first time I saw it on the trail to Mystic Falls, back during my summer working at Old Faithful. It doesn't offer direction. It offers a choice. Hike here or don't—just know the bear may or may not be around. Part of me wants to return to the safety of the road and give up hiking altogether. And part of me knows that is no way to live.

Our destination was the confluence of Hellroaring Creek and the Yellowstone River. Dad, a lover of the places where rivers converge, told us it looked like a beautiful spot for Jaime to fish, and that was what we intended to do. Well, Jaime intended to fish. I intended to read a book and listen to the river.

We considered our options. We could leave and hike somewhere else or—like the hikers who had parked the few other cars in the lot—accept that we were in bear country, check our bear spray, remind ourselves to pay attention, and forge ahead.

We'd already had a disturbing wildlife encounter that morning.

Two mule deer, probably yearlings, had emerged from the woods while we were gathering our gear. Rather than being scared off by our activity, they stood at the edge of the parking lot and watched us. After a while, the female approached our van. She walked to the back where Jaime was working, stuck her head inside, and started inspecting our stuff. Jaime shooed her away, but she didn't go far. When he resumed his work, she came back. Twice. After the third shooing, she switched her mark, circling around the van and attempting to climb in through the open passenger door where I was working.

Mountain mule deer seem smarter and less skittish than the Iowa white-tail I'm familiar with, although those who know deer tell me I'm wrong about the smarter part. Regardless, her interest in us was peculiar, so I examined them more closely. These two weren't just small. They were skinny, too—their ribs jutting out sharply. It was September, the end of summer's abundance. Their ribs shouldn't have been showing at all. These deer should have been plump, with reserves stored for the coming season of scarcity. The female shouldn't have been bold enough to approach us, let alone attempt to climb into our vehicle, and both of them should have been scared off by our presence—or at least our movement. I suppose they could have been sick. More likely, they'd been fed and, in their quest for more of the same, become habituated to humans. Now they were starving when they should have been thriving. They wouldn't survive the winter. It was heartbreaking.

Bear sign and disturbing wildlife encounter aside, Jaime and I decided to forge ahead with our hike.

The trail gave up six hundred feet of elevation almost immediately. At the base, we walked on level ground to one of the most unexpected sights I've seen in the backcountry: a steel suspension bridge in the wilderness. With its wooden planks and thick metal cables, it spans the Yellowstone River as it thunders through a deep and—by Yellowstone standards—narrow canyon. We paused halfway across to watch the water crash into the towering walls it had just been forced between and careen around bends in the canyon. We didn't linger in our usual way, though. Jaime had fishing to do.

Beyond the bridge, we walked into an open sage meadow and past a backcountry campsite—a *closed* backcountry campsite. I started to ask Jaime why he thought it was closed, and then I remembered the sign at the trailhead. We continued toward the confluence of the Yellowstone River and Hellroaring Creek where Jaime would fish and I would probably pretend to read while I actually watched for bears. I plodded along, occasionally settling down enough to enjoy the melody of the water and the whisper of dry grass. Jaime walked ahead of me because the trail was only wide enough for one person at a time. Whenever this was the case, he always placed himself in front in case we surprised a bear.

He stopped suddenly and turned around. "Let's head back."

"Why?" I asked.

"I just think we should go back."

I turned and walked back down the trail. "What's up?" I asked, knowing there was something he wasn't telling me.

"There was an elk skull buried in the trail. One of its antlers is sticking out of the ground," Jaime answered.

"Oh," I said, wishing I hadn't asked.

Bears sometimes bury carcasses for safekeeping between feedings. More disturbingly, they sometimes stay nearby, guarding their cache, so it's best to stay clear of their stowed food. We continued hiking single-file—probably more quietly than we should have. This time with Jaime in the back, stationed between me and the buried elk skull. If the bear came barreling out of the trees to protect its dinner, Jaime intended to be the one to get mauled.

That there was a skull buried in the trail is exactly the kind of information I want at the trailhead. But that's not how it works. Yellowstone is a wild place. Bells don't summon bears. Rangers don't pen the animals behind fences at night. And Siri—for now, at least—remains blessedly offline, unable to update me with the latest news or map out the safest route.

It's true on the trail and true in life. Rarely do I get to know what I want to know when I want to know it. Yellowstone's bear signs might not give me what I want, but they do offer what I need: a lesson in the art of walking in the wilderness, which is to say a lesson for living life. Pausing to consider the path before forging ahead, remembering to pay attention along the way, and being willing to course correct are all as necessary for living by faith as for walking in the wilderness.

25 DO-OVERS

Jaime and I set off down the path at a brisker-than-usual pace. Before long, and certainly sooner than I'd hoped, the trail to Monument Geyser Basin made good on its *short-but-steep* reputation. We'd been here before. This hike was something of a do-over from our first visit in 1995, back when we were inexperienced and unprepared for the drifts of wet spring snow we found on the trail. We hadn't even made it to where the ascent began before returning to our car, our shoes and pants soaked to the knees. Now we were back, on a quest to complete this trail that had been blocked by snow when we'd first visited Yellowstone years before.

We had some things in our favor. It was September, not May. The trail was clear of everything but the shadows that fell from the filtering pines. My knee was stronger, which made me more stable—thanks to the meniscus incident mentioned earlier that led to the repair of an old ACL injury. Over the course of three-and-a-half decades, I'd gone from being an unhappy hiker to a reluctant hiker to a happy hiker.

We also had a couple of things working against us. One was time, and the other was me. We had a deadline. And I don't have a high gear. I have one speed, and it's not fast. Beyond that, happy hiker or not, I have some commitment issues when it comes to the trail. It's still a little too easy for me to turn back on the steep ones —especially if there's something else I want to do. Which I did. Hence the deadline.

Our deadline involved a reservation for a tour at the Inn. This was unusual. Keeping a schedule was something we'd long since given up bothering with in Yellowstone. In the early years, we sometimes made dinner reservations. Over time, though, we decided we didn't want to cut our hikes short for artificial deadlines. We started eating out less so we could be on the trail more (and also so we could afford to visit the park more often). Along with that, we'd started camping more, which also contributed to more frequent visits and more time on the trail.

Monument is a small geyser basin set off in the woods at the end of a steep mile up the side of a hill. While we'd set off at a brisk pace, it wasn't long before I slowed down. There was no way I'd be keeping that pace at that grade all the way to the top. Still, I wanted to get there. I wanted to see what there was to see in this backcountry basin. Between our deadline and my speed and commitment issues, we weren't sure we'd get there to see it. But we wanted to try. So I kept on, strangely committed to doing whatever it took to reach the destination *and* make our reservation. Hiking faster than my natural pace and ignoring the complaints of my burning quads, I rounded one switchback after another. Somewhere along the way, my focus changed from seeing Monument for the sake of seeing Monument to just getting to Monument so we could turn around and move on to the next thing.

Even though it was only a mile, by the time we reached the top, my quads were threatening mutiny. Eventually, though, level ground, the familiar scent of sulfur in the air, and white wisps of vapor floating above the head-high trees signaled we were close, and we adopted a slower, more appreciative pace. Stepping through a narrow break in the wall of pines, I surveyed Monument's terrain with a single, sweeping glance. What I had expected was an active basin, teeming with colorful springs, bubbling pools, and hovering mist. What I found was a gray landscape that brought to mind a rooftop view of London during the Mary Poppins era.

I was underwhelmed. And because we had a deadline, we didn't linger. Immediately into the return trip, which we also took at a brisker-than-usual pace, disappointment set in. Yes, Monument had been less impressive than I had imagined. But I had been far less appreciative than it deserved. Monument was a geyser basin and therefore on the order of a miracle. Who was I to judge? There isn't even a scale for such things. I wanted to turn around and give it another go, but we had a deadline. There wasn't time.

Right about then, Jaime disappeared through a gap between the pines. Torn between appreciation for his curiosity and irritation at the potential delay, I followed. It didn't take long for me to find him—standing on a slim strip of exposed earth above the treetops. Here we lingered. Leaning against him, I surveyed the expansive view of the Gibbon Valley—the sporadic stands of lodgepole pines scattered across the meadow, the meandering Gibbon River winding through the fraying fall grass, and the feathery clouds flung across the late afternoon sky.

Everything in me relaxed. It wasn't the view. It was the *effect* of the view.

The wilderness speaks in unexpected ways, and on the little ledge that jutted out above the valley, I was still enough to hear. Our quest hadn't been what I'd thought. Monument may have been our goal, but this was our destination. We may have been hiking under a deadline, but the clock had done more than drive us.

Time had given us a gift.

The spot where we stood had been opened up by the Fires of 1988.[1] This is why the trees lining the trail were about my height.

---

1. Yellowstone's Summer of Fire is also known as the Fires of 1988—plural because

But the young lodgepole forest was growing. For now, I could see over the tops of the pines downslope from the ledge, but that wouldn't be true much longer. If Jaime's curiosity hadn't led us to this place, we would have missed this soul-stirring view, one that won't be there next time we take that hike.

I hope there is a next time because I want another do-over. I want to see Monument for what it is rather than what I expect it to be. But if I never take this trail again, it shifted my thinking—and therefore my course—and for that I am grateful.

---

there wasn't just one fire, there were nearly 250. They burned for months, consistently gaining ground more rapidly than they could be contained by firefighters While video footage of raging wildfires is common today, this was not the case back then. Every day my family and I watched the nightly news coverage of flames that eventually devoured more than a third of the park's 2.2 million acres. We listened to reporters predict the end of Yellowstone as we knew it. And we wondered. *What would be left?* On this side of the fire, it's as obvious that the prophecies were wrong as it is possible to understand why they were made. I've included three books about the fires and what followed on the Resources and Reading list

YELLOWSTONE NATIONAL PARK

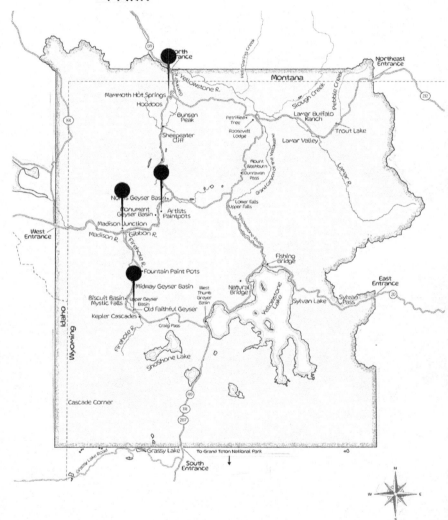

26 WHAT THE WILDERNESS DOES

"Are you okay? You seem kind of... Well, kind of..." I trailed off, uncertain how to land my observation.

"Tired?" Jaime offered.

I didn't have a word ready to describe Jaime's out-of-character behavior. I decided to go with his *tired*.

"It's been a long day," he said.

That it had. We'd left home at 4 o'clock that morning —Saturday morning, a change from our traditional Friday night as-soon-as-Jaime-got-home-from-work departure. The kids and I were in various stages of recovering from Influenza A. Jaime and I had vacillated over whether or not to set off on this trip at all, but life had taught us that illnesses—strep throat, pneumonia, and influenza among them—find us on the road as easily as at home. Between reservations for three lodges and in-park oversnow transportation, rescheduling wasn't an option. So we left for Yellowstone after one extra, albeit short, night of sleep in our own beds.

All this resulted in the seething stranger who had shared our booth at the Burger King in Billings, Montana. Because Jaime was more of a sower of peace and stability in our family than a spreader of stress, the kids and I peeked surreptitiously at each other, mystified as we followed him through the wintry air toward our vehicle.

Jaime drove across the snowy parking lot and paused—noticeably longer than he needed to—at the stop sign. It was one of those baffling intersections that requires travelers to turn away from the interstate, drive deeper into town, and make a U-turn just to get back to the on-ramp. But Jaime didn't turn right, as the sign dictated. He shot straight across, launching us up and over the median, turned left, and proceeded to I- 90.

No. *Tired* didn't quite cover it.

Two hours down the road, Jaime broke into my intermittent sleep. "How are you doing? I know you're worn out from being sick, but I don't think I should drive anymore. Can you? We're about an hour from the park."

It was time for my standard anemic hour behind the wheel. Even in his exhausted state, Jaime waited to ask me to drive until that was all that was left.

I opened the passenger door and scurried around the back of the vehicle where Jaime and I—either because we were too cold or too tired—skipped our customary kiss-in-passing. I climbed into the driver's seat. It was ten o'clock. The thermometer on the rearview mirror read fourteen degrees.

"Thanks," Jaime murmured. His eyes were closed before I pulled back onto the highway that would take us into the park.

I drove straight into a feisty wind that soon delivered heavy snow, the sort that would have floated straight down had it not been whipped into a blinding frenzy. As we crept along, I watched the temperature reading. Like the snow, it was falling. Fast. It plummeted twenty-nine degrees before stopping at fifteen below.

The wind and snow vanished as suddenly as they appeared, leaving an open highway and nothing for me to concern myself with but the occasional curve. One degree at a time, the temperature gauge regained the twenty-nine it had lost. At a bend in the road, I entered a low-lying cloud that went on for miles. Slowing again, I drove tentatively through the misty veil until it, too, disappeared and I emerged into a clear, dark night and the comfort of the open road.

It didn't last.

Within minutes, the wind picked up again, bringing swirling snow and plunging temperatures. After revisiting the fifteen-below mark, the air cleared and returned to a balmy fourteen degrees above. Relieved, I drove a few carefree miles before clouds once again engulfed the road. By the time the cloak lifted, we'd arrived at the outskirts of Gardiner, Montana, the gateway community at Yellowstone's North Entrance. I drove the remaining six miles over a clear road and pulled up under the awning at the Mammoth Hot Springs Hotel at 12:30 Sunday morning.

I touched Jaime's leg. He didn't move. "Hey Babe," I whispered, "we're here."

He opened his eyes and pulled himself upright. "How was the drive?"

We'd been apprehensive about the kids when we planned this trip. Only Emma was anywhere near as young as we'd imagined when we'd first talked about bringing them to the park in the snowy season. When my parents brought Matt and me to Yellowstone in the winter, we'd rented snowmobiles to explore the park. Snowmobile rental had always been expensive, but with changes to winter use policies, it had become more so. No longer could an individual or a family simply set out into the park on a motorized sled—whether rented or owned—unattended. All snowmobilers were required to be accompanied by a guide. The cost of renting three machines, which a family of our size required, plus the guide, put snowmobiling outside what we felt comfortable paying for a family vacation—even a special one. We worried that the kids would be disappointed.

They burst out of the hotel into a light snow that first morning. Jaime and I followed them over the shoveled sidewalks and quiet roads of the Mammoth Hot Springs settlement, past Officer's Row and the Albright Visitor Center. They were ready to see Yellowstone in a new season. They knew spring's baby bison, long days, and remnants of winter. They knew summer's crowds, brilliant wildflowers, and chaotic traffic. They knew autumn's bugling bull elk, bright afternoons, crisp mornings, and unexpected snowfalls.

They knew winter and they knew Yellowstone, but they'd never seen them together.

After breakfast, we got into the vehicle, drove a couple of miles up the road, parked right outside Mammoth's upper terraces, and pulled our gear out of the back of the vehicle. We'd snowshoed together at home, once, over powder that wasn't very deep. The gently rolling, reasonably short Upper Terrace Loop was a test to determine whether we'd attempt a longer, more challenging trek down at Old Faithful.

We set out over packed snow. Before long, our path—a one-way road open only to snowshoers and cross-country skiers— began to climb, an ascent that elicited no complaints. Even Emma, who was less tolerant of the ups and downs of mountain terrain than the rest of us, offered no objections. The view from the top opened up over the entire Mammoth area, its steamy springs, streets, and buildings all nestled together under a sunny sky.

We trekked uphill and down, past deer and rivulets of thermal runoff, through the silence of sound-absorbing snow. And the only sound to be absorbed? Conversation, laughter, and the thud of the occasional snowball.

The kids were not disappointed.

"Where's Dad?" I asked the next morning.

"I think he took the stuff we don't need to the vehicle," Mason said.

The stuff in question would be the bags and totes we'd spent the morning sorting and repacking, the five of us tripping over each other in a tiny hotel room filled with clothes and winter gear, all in the name of getting ourselves, our snowshoes, poles, and luggage to the appointed meeting place by 7:30 that morning. Seven-thirty isn't early. We only had to walk down the corridor, through the lobby, and out the door. We didn't have to leave time for security checks. But while I am a morning person, we are not a morning family. And every decision, every movement of an item from one bag to another, every bite of breakfast took longer—much longer—than it should have.

At least it seemed that way to Jaime.

The kids and I were standing near a small sea of people and suitcases outside the Mammoth Hot Springs Hotel. The bags were waiting to be tossed onto a wagonesque conveyance attached to a vehicle similar to the bombardier that had ferried Jaime and me north from Flagg Ranch to the Old Faithful Snow Lodge a decade before. As was true then, Yellowstone's interior roads were open only to oversnow vehicles. The people, all attired for winter's worst, waited to board a bus that would take us just a few miles deeper into the park to the end of the paved road where we would board snowcoaches for the trip to Old Faithful.

I looked at our pile of bags. Like most of the other suitcases, they were black. Unlike the others, ours were without white tags.

"What do you suppose those tags are?" I asked.

"What tags?" asked Jaime as he walked up behind me.

"Those." I pointed.

Still fatigued from the drive and stressed from the hectic morning, he pivoted and stalked back into the hotel, returning a moment later with a fistful of tags and a couple of pens. "Here. Start filling these out."

"These" were baggage tickets. We should have received them at check-in, but because we had arrived so late, we did not. By the time our tags were filled out, affixed to our suitcases, and delivered to the luggage transport, we were the last ones to board the bus.

"The worst part of getting older is that I can't take time pressure anymore," Jaime said as he sank into his seat at the back of the bus.

"Well, Babe, you can relax now. The luggage is loaded and so are we."

He gave me a grim look. "I'm trying."

The bus took us not far beyond the Upper Terrace Loop where we had snowshoed the previous morning. Just before reaching the gate that separated the plowed asphalt from the groomed snow, the bus turned onto a service road and deposited us in front of a little wooden depot. Standing on a patch of packed snow, we waited with our fellow travelers to be summoned to our next vehicle. Uniformed drivers called name after name until there were only a few of us left.

"Ogbourne," a chipper young man called out. We were the final five of his eleven passengers.

Elyse joined two people in the second-to-the-last seat, and the remaining four of us wedged ourselves onto the back bench. Jaime sat in silence next to me as we waited for everyone to fasten their seat belts so we could depart. I smiled at him. He stared blankly back at me. It was eight o'clock in the morning, and he looked ready for bed.

"We made it," I said, taking his hand. "It's going to be okay."

"I know," Jaime said. "I hate getting old."

He looked out the window at the lacy trees lining the road. Before long he was smiling. This is what the wilderness does. It restores our souls, trading our weariness for wonder.

27 OCEANS OF SNOW

Not far down the groomed road where our snowcoach joined the long caravan heading into the park's interior, we came to a slow stop. Bison. *I should have known.*

They were trotting toward us, shoulder to shoulder across the width of the road. Most of them ambled right past, but a few became disoriented and turned in the opposite direction. With their heads to their companions and their tails to our snowcoach, they spread across our lane and stood like a row of linemen, each uniformed by a buildup of fine snow that fell from the overcast sky.

Had we been on snowmobiles, I'm not sure I would have had the courage to continue. But we weren't on snowmobiles. We were in a snowcoach, sequestered behind a fiberglass shield that even the strongest bison could only dent.

Eventually, most of the herd made its way past us, and the few confused stragglers blocking our way righted themselves. Our driver edged forward a few inches at a time, herding the bison toward the other lane. Of the many bison we saw that day, these were the only ones on the road. The rest kept their distance, small herds dotted throughout the meadows, hip-deep in snow, their heads buried in search of sustenance.

Our destination was the Old Faithful Snow Lodge, deep in the park and about as far from Mammoth Hot Springs as the figure-eight road reached. It wasn't long before we passed into Yellowstone's stark winter monochrome, a contrast to Mammoth's more subtle palette. Here in the white and evergreen-dominated landscape, the snow softened craggy peaks and blurred the lines between mountaintops and the cloudy sky. Pines, their boughs peeking out from beneath frosty lace, reflected in the rivers that ran through drifted meadows.

We stopped at Norris Geyser Basin, not to explore but in case anyone required a stop at a cold and comfortless comfort station. Our family exited along with everyone else but spent the time examining the exterior of the vehicle rather than braving the unheated bathroom. This snowcoach was no bombardier. The historic fleet had been retired the winter before, replaced by quiet, cozy twelve-passenger vans that could quickly and easily be converted each year for oversnow travel. Instead of long skis out front and a large track underneath, the van had small, triangular tracks that fit in each of the four wheel wells. Wheels at the base of the tread propelled it along, collecting frost and creating spiky icicles that radiated from their centers—each one unique, and lovely as a snowflake.

A few miles past Norris, our driver, who did as good a job giving a tour as transporting us safely from one place to the next, slowed down and pulled over. "We're coming up on the Chocolate Pots on the right," he called back.

On the far bank of the Gibbon River, there was a break in the snow cover. Warmed by thermal activity above and below the ground, the snow had melted, revealing a spring surrounded by rich, cocoa-colored soil and mineral deposits reminiscent of caramel topping. We'd driven this road dozens of times, yet we'd never noticed this feature. Blending with the brown hues of the fall forest, it was hidden in autumn. In winter, though, it was highlighted by the surrounding white and impossible to miss.

"There's a swan up ahead," our driver said after he'd driven a few more miles down the road. "Yellowstone has eleven resident trumpeter swans this year. There are more than that right now, though, because of the ones that migrate in for the winter."

True to his role as guide, he eased to a stop while we searched the river bank. But it wasn't just a single swan. There were three, two adults and a gray cygnet. Between the blurring effect of the falling snow, the undulating curves of the drifts, and the graceful arcs of the swans' necks, none of them were easy to find. Swimming upstream, they foraged for the aquatic flora and fauna that make up their diet.

When he left the main road to pull in at Madison, everyone exited the snowcoaches once again. Madison not only had a warming hut for snowmobilers and cross-country skiers, it also boasted heated bathrooms with flush toilets. The line was long, and so was the stop. Tired of sitting, the girls and I meandered around, stretching our legs in the fresh, cold air.

"Do you know where Daddy and Mason are?" I asked when our companions began boarding the snowcoaches.

"I think they walked down to the river," Elyse said.

Instantly panicked, I told the girls, "I'll be right back. You go ahead and get in the snowcoach."

With Jaime and Mason under the influence of the river, to be "right back" would require a miracle. First I had to find them, which was a problem. While I knew exactly where they would be —at the confluence of the Gibbon and the Firehole—I didn't know exactly where that was located or how far away it was. On top of that, I was going to have to navigate snow that was several feet deep.

Turning toward the river, I scurried across the groomed surface. When I found a trail of broken snow leaving the parking lot, I followed it—unconcerned, for once, about bears. They were hibernating. What worried me was how far downstream Jaime and Mason had wandered. I pictured them standing where the Firehole and the Gibbon came together—the birthplace of the Madison.

Three rivers. Three books for Jaime to read. Time and distance would mean nothing to him in such a place. Panicked though I was, this is who he was, and this is why we were here: to show the kids and see for ourselves what Yellowstone was in a different season. I found them faster than I thought I would, standing exactly as I had imagined them—together at the water's edge. While I wasn't exactly "right back," we managed to board before all the other snowcoaches departed.

The road we were traveling paralleled the Firehole River, a bolt of blue unwinding from one geyser basin to the next. Our driver pointed out a bald eagle soaring against the gray sky. "Some of Yellowstone's eagles," he told us, "stay in the park year-round, but a lot of them migrate further west for the winter, and some come down from Canada for the season. Like the swans, bald eagles come for the open rivers so they can hunt for fish and waterbirds. Golden eagles prefer places like the Hayden or Lamar Valleys, where there is open space for hunting small animals."

As we made the final part of our journey to the Old Faithful Snow Lodge, I looked out at the Yellowstone landscape. I knew this place. I knew the verdure of spring, the vibrant wildflowers of summer, and the faded grasses of fall. I even knew this stark wintry canvas with its bison trotting down the road and dotted across oceans of snow. Familiar yet always foreign, Yellowstone's wilderness had new things to show and old things to reveal in novel ways. Perhaps our family wasn't that different from the migratory swans and eagles that returned to Yellowstone year after year. They came to fill their bellies. We came to fill our hearts and souls and to restore our minds and bodies.

28 A SEASON FOR EVERYTHING

The next day dawned cold—and not only in comparison to the more temperate Mammoth Hot Springs. A polar vortex had plummeted temperatures park-wide. Exposing as little skin as possible, we emerged into the gloom of a still, cheerless morning. The temperature had risen only five degrees from the overnight low of twenty below, complicating the chore of strapping our snowshoes to our boots. It wasn't something we could do while wearing gloves, and our fingers became unresponsive almost as soon as they were exposed to the arctic air. Chilled and clumsy though we were, we finished the job and set off across the groomed roadway into a day that taught me the difference between mountain cold and Midwest cold. Yellowstone's arid air carries little moisture, even in winter. Iowa is humid year-round. While our fingers did not function well in the frigid air, on that windless day, fifteen degrees below zero in Yellowstone felt balmy compared with fifteen above at home.

Our destination was Observation Point, via a short trail that begins on the far side of Old Faithful. From the trailhead, it's only a half-mile up through the woods to a panoramic view of the Upper Geyser Basin, including Old Faithful and the Inn. While it's short, it's also switchbacked, and trail guide writers call it strenuous. They don't lie. In temperate weather, or at least when there isn't snow on the ground, it's a thirty-minute, thigh-burning haul up a wooded slope that delivers you to a clearing two hundred fifty feet above Old Faithful.

It isn't too tough, but everything is harder in winter.

While our family hikes this trail regularly, only Jaime and I had ever attempted it on snowshoes, and only Jaime had succeeded. That was before the surgery that made my knees more mountain-worthy, and I hadn't made it to the top. I waited at a spot with something of a view while Jaime sprinted the rest of the way, arriving in time to see Old Faithful erupt.

We hoped that everyone would make it this time, but we weren't sure. The kids were all old enough but, before our easy trek through the Upper Terrace at Mammoth earlier in the week, only Mason actually liked snowshoeing. Elyse was always happy just to be together, no matter what we were doing. As was the case at Mammoth Hot Springs, our chief concern was Emma. Her history of hiking happily even in warm weather was checkered, at best.

Uncertain about reaching our destination, off we set into the subzero day, checking the next predicted eruption time at the Visitor Education Center along the way. It would be about an hour, plus or minus ten minutes. We continued to the far side of Old Faithful, where we left the boardwalk and entered the woods. Before long, we stopped on a stout wooden bridge to search for trout and otters in the Firehole's temperate water. Jaime and I had seen both from this bridge in winter before. Today, though, we saw no wildlife. Still, we enjoyed the melody of the river and the rising mist from the Upper Geyser Basin.

Not far beyond the bridge, the trail began to climb. Mason led the way, followed by Elyse and me. Emma trailed a little farther behind, and Jaime took his place in the back, relishing his role as what hikers call the sweeper—watching out for his family and making sure no one got left behind. Though the orange trail blazes stood out against the white backdrop, they were unnecessary. Even under eight inches of freshly fallen snow, the trench through the powder made the trail easy to find. We ascended the switchbacked path, able to see—as is often the case—nothing but the surrounding trees. Then, at a bend in the trail, the forest opened, presenting us with a sweeping vista of the valley below—shrouded in steam and surrounded by lacy green trees on every side. Searing through the clouds, the sun created an intense halo bent on burning away the morning mist. We stopped to absorb the scene, removing hoods, hats, and goggles that had trapped the body heat generated by the climb.

We made it—all of us—to Observation Point. According to the clock and the crowd gathered on the boardwalk below, Old Faithful was due to erupt soon. As we waited in the arctic air, we put on our hats and our goggles, pulled up our hoods, and began to shift from one cold foot to the other.

"When are we going back down?" Emma asked. "I'm cold."

We wanted the kids to see a winter eruption so we put her off. It wasn't long, though, before Jaime decided we'd stood long enough in the subzero weather. "One more minute," he said.

After an eruption-less minute, we returned to the trail. When we stepped from the woods, Old Faithful was still steaming and the crowd was still waiting. We joined them on the boardwalk.

"When are we going back to the Snow Lodge?" Emma asked again. "I'm cold."

"I'll go with her," I offered.

"Oh good!" said Emma. "Do you want to ice skate when we get back?"

"Ice skate? I thought you were cold."

"I am, Mommy. But I won't be cold when I'm skating."[1]

---

1. During the winter, the Old Faithful Snow Lodge and Mammoth Hot Springs Hotel each feature a small, outdoor skating rink—complete with lights and a blazing fire. Add a snowfall, and the experience is pure delight. I've heard it takes 150 hours of labor to build each rink, a project that begins as early as mid-October.

By one o'clock we were in the packed twelve-passenger van for the return trip to Mammoth. Same seats, different driver—a talkative one. Like Jaime, he was a fly fisherman.

"So you were here last fall, when the park had to close because of the government shutdown?" I asked.

"Yeah, I was," he said.

"So what did you do? How did getting everyone out of the park work?" I had wondered about this when it happened because some years a good number of concessionaire employees come from Eastern Europe and Asia. They couldn't exactly drive home —or even to the airport.

"Well, not everyone was able to leave, or had to leave, depending on how you look at it. We couldn't get everything done at the marina before the park closed, so I stayed."

"You got to stay?" asked Elyse, awed. She, along with her siblings, her cousins, and my parents, had been forced to leave Theodore Roosevelt National Park a few years before due to a shutdown.

"Yep. I stayed. I'd been waiting all season for some good, quiet fall fly fishing." I envisioned him out on the Firehole, alone without another fisherman in sight. "I'd been waiting all fall," he continued, "but I didn't get to fish."

"Why not?" I asked.

"Because the park was closed. The employees who had to stay weren't allowed to do anything recreational. I was here, but I couldn't fish. It was hard."

Knowing my fly fisherman, I imagined it would have been.

"There's a cow elk up ahead on that hillside," our driver said, changing the subject. There she was, nose down in the snow, the same soft brown as the rocks peeking through the snow behind her. We stopped. She pulled her head from the snow and looked our way. "This is unusual," the driver observed. "She's oriented downhill with her front feet and head lower than her rear feet and backside. Usually, elk graze with their head uphill."

With that, it became clear why we had all those pictures of elk hindquarters.

Not far down the road, the van slowed again. "Do you see anything?" I asked Jaime.

He looked around and shook his head. "No, unless we're pulling in at Fountain Paint Pot. It's up ahead."

I wrinkled my nose. "Why would we do that?"

Before long we were exiting the van. Sighing, I joined the rest of the group making the long trudge from the Fountain Paint Pot parking lot up the sloping, snow-covered boardwalk toward the first thermal feature.

Jaime and I had made this walk once before, under a scorching July sun, when we were here with my parents and Matt and his wife. That had been twenty years before, and we'd never felt the need to stop again. Every time we drive past and see the masses moving from the crowded parking lot toward the bleak plain to join the snaking line of people on the boardwalk, I have an urge to open my window and shout, "Turn back! Drive on! There are better things to see up ahead."

It wasn't that we didn't like paint pots. We'd just never taken to these particular paint pots. We preferred Artist Paint Pots, which our family started referring to as the Frog Pots when the kids were young.

Paint pots are thermal features that occur in places where water is limited and gas is plentiful. The gas breaks down the surrounding rock, giving color and body to the small amount of water present. Subject to seasonal changes in moisture, spring generally finds them thin and watery, and late summer and fall see them thick and gooey.

When Jaime and I first visited Yellowstone, we parked on the empty asphalt strip masquerading as a parking lot for Artist Paint Pots and set off down the narrow dirt trail to see what was there. What was there was a lone bison blocking the path. Thwarted, we moved on. When we returned the next day the bison was gone, but the little lot was packed with vehicles, most with their rear bumpers protruding into passing traffic. We wedged our little red Plymouth Sundance into a spot and discovered a new favorite place.

Today, the tiny parking strip and narrow path have been replaced by a long drive and large lot. A looping trail cuts through thick, young lodge-pole pine forest, mostly regrowth from the Fires of 1988. We always turn left and walk past a variety of watery yet palette-worthy thermal features toward the thick, neutral-tinted mud pots beyond. These are the Frog Pots, features our kids sat beside for long stretches of time, content to watch the viscous bubbles burst. These bubbles, created by the release of gas rather than the action of boiling, packed serious velocity, often causing them to fling out in the shape of a jumping frog.

The Frog Pots, however, were not where our guide was taking us.

Still wondering why we would stop here, I dutifully followed the guide up the boardwalk. When he stopped, I halted with the group and studied the closest feature: Celestine Spring. Deep blue water pooled in the greige-hued ground common to the geyser basins. Even in the bitter cold of a Yellowstone winter, Celestine Spring sheltered a temperate region—a tiny, lavish rainforest boasting lush tufts of thriving, vibrant moss enveloped between the extremes of scalding water and arctic air. I had to admit the ring of snow added some charm, as did the surrounding flocked forest. Gazing into the spring and the microclimate it created, I felt the familiar chagrin of realizing, once again, that I was judging a miracle. All twelve of us walked the remainder of the boardwalk in reverent silence broken only occasionally by our previously talkative guide. Mist created by the clash of disparate temperatures clung to everything we passed—the railings, the rocks, the trees—gracing it all with a delicate overlay of hoarfrost.

My instinct not to stop here had been in every way wrong.

Left to myself, I wouldn't have stopped at Fountain Paint Pot.

I would have held out for something better. And I would have missed the stark, exquisite display—not only of the harsh contrast of heat and cold but also of the grace that resides in the misty land in the middle. But I wasn't left to myself. I was, once again, under the care of a guide leading me through a place I didn't want to go where winter's wilderness proved what I struggle to believe: There is a season for everything, and all things are beautiful in their time.

YELLOWSTONE NATIONAL PARK

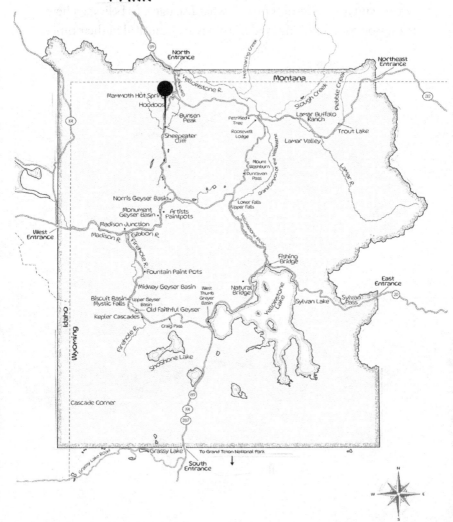

29 PRIORITIES

Jaime tapped the brake and engaged the turn signal.
"What are we doing?" I asked. We didn't need gas. He'd filled up at the last stop.
"Pulling over."
He took a right at the top of the off-ramp, drove a few yards, and turned right again, this time down a long gravel lane that paralleled I-90. When he pointed toward a picnic table shaded by the spreading branches of an aged tree, I knew exactly what we were doing. We were stopping. Sixty miles of silence was enough. Especially over Mountain Dew.

It had started at what should have been a quick stop at Cabela's. We didn't need much. We could have been in and out in a few minutes, but we'd wandered around and squandered time that should have been devoted to driving the remaining seven hours to where we wanted to be: Chico Hot Springs Resort in Pray, Montana.

At least, Chico is where I wanted to be.

An hour from Yellowstone's North Entrance, it was our day's destination. First opened as a hotel in 1900, it later became a health spa, then a hospital, and finally a resort. In its early days, people came for the water. Soaking in either of its two hot spring-fed pools was said to heal myriad maladies, including those of the skin, kidneys, and blood. Today, people go for recreation and relaxation. For our family, Chico is an antidote and a reward for long hours in the car. At ninety-six degrees—give or take, depending on the day—the spacious main swimming pool is roomy enough for the kids, warm enough for me, and capable of cloaking the entire courtyard in mist on cool evenings. The inflow from the hot springs is enough to fill and drain the two pools three times every day. While fresh, thermal water flows through continuously, at closing time each night the pools are completely drained. By seven the next morning, they're full.

We'd been making good time and were on target to arrive at Chico in the afternoon. I didn't want to waste any more of it than we needed to—at Cabela's or anywhere else. I wanted to get on the road so we could get out of the vehicle and into the water. So when we finally got out of the store and Jaime started stacking suitcases on the pavement behind the vehicle, I felt our early arrival and relaxing evening draining away like water from Chico's pools.

"What are you doing?" I asked Jaime.

"Getting a Mountain Dew."

"Why?" That was the verbalized question. What I meant was this: *Why would you waste time digging for Mountain Dew when we could be on the road?*

"Because I always have a Mountain Dew in the middle of the day, and I'm thirsty."

"Can you wait for lunch? It's already eleven, and you know it won't be long before the kids are hungry. If you get it then, we won't have to take time to do all this twice. There's water up front."

By now the picnic tote was on the concrete next to the suitcases, and Jaime was extracting the cooler. I stalked to my seat, climbed in, and slammed the door. It was morning, and Chico was only seven hours away. At this rate, I was certain the pool would be closed by the time we arrived.

So after those sixty miles of silence, Jaime parked under the canopy of an old oak and we fixed the fallout from the Cabela's stop. Once the five of us finished eating a picnic lunch in the shade, Jaime asked me to drive. For once, I drove more than my usual hour. I drove a lot of them. While I'd like to say it was because I was motivated to get to Chico, more likely it was because we were traveling in our new-to-us Toyota Sequoia. We'd had it less than a month, and it had changed the whole driving experience for me.

It felt like a tank. It sat high enough that I could actually see. For the first time in all my years of driving, I was using my mirrors. It was delightful. With Jaime sleeping beside me and the kids working their way through their books in the back seat, I calculated how long it would take to cover the distance between where we were and where we were headed at seventy-five miles per hour. We were still making good time. I relaxed— as much as a flatlander navigating an interstate carved into the side of a mountain can. And then, as I approached a bend in the road, a jolt interrupted my countdown to our arrival at Chico.

"What was that?" I took my foot off of the accelerator. "Did something hit us?"

Jaime blinked bleary eyes. "I don't know. Maybe."

I searched the reflection in the rearview mirror. Maybe I'd hit one of the dreaded fallen rocks that have earned themselves warning signs all over the mountain west. As I looked, a sedan emerged from my blind spot. The driver, a gal with long, brunette hair, moved ahead of us, turned on her blinker, and pulled over. Based on the divot across her passenger side doors, I surmised that she was the something that had hit us.

"Do you think she was texting?" I asked.

"Did somebody hit us?" Emma asked.

"Yes, but it's all going to be okay. You're all okay, right?"

The kids nodded in unison, and I eased to a stop. No land, not even a ditch, extended beyond the slim strip of earth that served as the shoulder. Jaime got out and slithered along our passenger side.

"I'm sorry," the woman wailed as Jaime made his way between our vehicle and hers. "I'm traveling for work and I'm sick and I took some medicine. I guess I fell asleep."

Jaime tried to interrupt her lamentations, but she would have none of it. She was sorry. She fell asleep. It was her fault.

Jaime tried again. "This isn't a safe place to stop. We're not far enough off the road because there isn't much shoulder."

She carried on.

Jaime broke in. "It's okay, but we need to move. We're on a curve. The cars heading this way are driving into the sun and can't see us. It's dangerous. Follow us to the off-ramp. We can talk there."

She finally calmed down enough for both her and Jaime to return to their vehicles, drive to the ramp, and park in the little lot at the top to exchange insurance information. The kids and I watched for a while, but watching people exchange insurance information is boring. The kids returned to their books, and I got out.

"I'm so sorry," she wailed again.

"It's okay," I said.

"Your car is broken, and I've ruined your beautiful vacation."

I smiled at her. "The other doors still work. No one was hurt. Nothing is ruined. It's okay."

And it was. We were alive. She was alive. No one was even hurt. Those were the important things. More important than getting to Chico.

Jaime was almost back at the vehicle when she called, "Thank you for not yelling at me."

Jaime slid into the driver's seat to complete our journey to Chico. Along the way, I watched the passing scenery and contemplated my priorities.

30 THE WEIGHT OF THE WILDERNESS

When Emma turned four, she was old enough to join her dad and her siblings for a little rock scrambling.

"What did you think?" I asked as we walked, hand in hand, back to the van.

"I got kind of scared," she told me. "But then I remembered the Bible."

That was not the answer I expected. "Oh. What did you remember about the Bible?"

"It says we don't need to be afraid because God is always with us, so I wasn't afraid."

She made it sound so easy.

Four years later, a few days after our mountainside car accident, I'd committed to tagging along on their quest to scale the rustic stairs up Sheepeater Cliff. After I was no longer able to hide behind pregnancies, babies, and toddlers, I excused myself in the name of making lunch for as many years as the kids had allowed. While I wasn't afraid of heights, I wasn't particularly stable or strong. The potential for embarrassing myself in some way was real, so I wasn't exactly looking forward to scrambling up the cliff. However, in the spirit of family togetherness, I agreed to join them.

Still, a cloud of anxiety had been following me all morning—from Chico, into the park, and down the road to the columnar basalt cliff that awaited me.

On the far side of the entrance to the Sheepeater Cliff Picnic Area, the road was littered with haphazardly abandoned vehicles. "Looks like a bear jam. Or maybe a really good elk," I said.

"Do you want to check it out?" Jaime asked.

I considered. Stopping would delay my climb to the top of the cliff. It was autumn, the height of the elk rut. Bull elk were everywhere, surrounded not only by their harems but also by an entourage of humans. The elk we enjoyed; it was the crowd around them we'd wearied of.

"No. Let's go on," I said, meaning something more along the lines of *Let's get this over with.*

Like most of Yellowstone's picnic areas, Sheepeater Cliff is home to only a handful of tables scattered among the trees. More often than not, we're alone, or nearly so. Not that day, though. That day there were people. Plenty of them. A Yellowstone Association minibus was parked in the lot, its class gathered along the bank of the Gardner River and its driver waiting at a picnic table.[1] Two groups dined at others. Jaime and I released the kids to explore the tumbled rocks at the base of the cliff while we carted our supplies to a table off to the side. I surveyed the rest of the people spread throughout the picnic area and hoped they'd be gone when we finished our lunch.

Columnar basalt is a volcanic rock that cools into columns resembling ranks of soldiers waiting to take their turn at the front line. Over time these columns break apart into tidy blocks, creating a natural staircase in the forest. These steps call to my climbing husband and our kids, but I tend to trip even on stan-

---

1. Yellowstone Association is now a part of Yellowstone Forever, an organization that provides both educational programming for visitors and philanthropic opportunities to support Yellowstone National Park.

dard, handrailed stairs in the civilized world and was not interested in witnesses.

Mason and Elyse climbed up and down the face of the cliff. Emma flitted back and forth between them and a path she'd discovered around the side, a dirt trail each of the kids traveled when they were tiny, safe in the arms of Jaime or my dad. After making everyone's sandwiches, Jaime and I called the kids for lunch. Even with the time it took to consume and clear it away, not one of the other picnickers had departed.

There were going to be witnesses.

"I'm taking my trail around the easy way, Mama. You can come with me," Emma said in a tempting final bid to save me.

"Thanks, Girlie, but I said I'd climb to the top, and that's what I'm going to do." I trudged behind Jaime, Mason, and Elyse, hoping no one at the picnic tables would pay attention to the mountain goaty family helping the middle-aged woman up the face of the cliff.

Aside from negotiating a couple of blocks that hadn't yet broken down into a manageable size, the worst part was picking my way over the ones jumbled together at the base. The actual climbing of the stone staircase wasn't too bad—until I remembered the witnesses, turned around, and discovered they were watching. *Of course.* Today, of all days, none of the picnickers seemed to be in a hurry. Sighing, I hoisted myself up over the edge, crawled onto my knees, and hauled myself into a respectable position. Jaime, Elyse, and Emma were all waiting for me. Mason was a hundred feet away already, across from us in the meadow. Unlike them, I'd never been there before so I scanned the scenery from right to left, ending where Emma's easy way had only moments before deposited her onto the grassy plateau where we stood.

Barely visible between the trunks and boughs of the lodgepole trees that surrounded the meadow, something was moving on Emma's path. Something with a big, brown, shaggy head wagging back and forth. *There's a bison.* I thought. *What would a bison be doing up here?* (This was a ridiculous question. Bison can be anywhere in Yellowstone. Anytime.) Then it crested the hill and lumbered into the clearing.

"Oh! It's a bear!" I exclaimed—excited, as always, by the sight of a bear. Then it registered how close we were to it, or it was to us. "Oh," I whispered, shocked. "It's a bear."

Jaime's eyes followed my gaze.

"You've got a griz," called one of the witnesses from the picnic area below.

A griz? We were in trouble. I looked for cubs. If we had popped up between a mama bear and her young, we weren't just in trouble, one of us was probably dead.

"Mason," Jaime called in a low voice. After he got Mason's attention, he pointed at the bear and then the ground in front of us.

"I don't see any cubs," I told Jaime.

Emma gasped. "Cubs? There's a bear? I'm scared!" she announced as she turned and started to run. I clamped my hand on her shoulder and fought the temptation to remind her that when we run from an animal we look like something they should chase.

Emma wasn't the only one who was scared. I was too. But we had work to do, and I focused on that. Protocol for a surprise bear encounter is to slowly back away—something easier said than done, and also something our location on the edge of a cliff prevented. Since that wasn't an option, I turned to climb back down the way we had come up. It seemed like the fastest way to get out of the way, which is what we needed to do.

"No," Jaime said. After two decades of marriage, he was well acquainted with my lack of athletic ability and knew climbing back down would not end well. "Follow me." He looked at Mason. "You know the way down the other side, don't you?" Mason nodded. "You take the front and lead us down. Girls, follow Mason. I'll take the rear."

"Are you sure that's a good idea?" I asked.

"We can't stay here, and we can't climb down the cliff. It's a black, not a griz, and it doesn't seem to be bothered by us right now."

He lowered his voice. "Nat, if the bear charges, you take the kids and keep going."

"What?" I protested, appalled. "We can't just leave you."

"Take the kids and keep moving."

With less than twenty-five yards between us and the bear, we set off single file down the trail toward the trees on the far side. Mason took the lead, followed by Elyse, then Emma, me, Jaime, and the bear, who seemed to be taking the same path we were.

That joke, the one where you don't need to outrun the bear, you only need to outrun the guy behind you, disintegrates completely when the guy behind you is your husband, the father of your children, the one you'd really like to go home with till death do you part—and you'd prefer death arrive later rather than sooner and not involve a bear.

"Mason," I asked. "Is it still back there?" We'd taken maybe fifteen steps.

Stable son of his father, he turned around mid-stride. "Yeah, Mom, it's still back there."

"Is what back there?" asked Elyse who, without asking even one question, had immediately gotten in line and followed Mason.

"A bear," I told her, offering no parental reassurance.

"Oh," she shuddered. "There's a bear."

Jaime did better. "It's okay, Elyse. Mason knows the way down, and Mom and I are right behind you. Just keep going."

The trail across the top of the cliff stretched on and on ahead of us, and we all kept walking and walking, as quickly as we could while keeping a measured pace. The bear did the same, only more quickly than us. With a body built for the terrain, he gained on us constantly. Too often I asked Mason if he was still back there, which he always was. Too often I wondered why we'd left our bear spray sitting in the vehicle. And too often I thought about the people in the picnic area. They knew we were up there with a bear, but just as when the couple on the snowmobile had stopped and waited until our face-off with the bison had ended, there was nothing they could do but watch. We were on our own.

We left the cliff top and began to descend the slope, picking our way through the woods with its boulders and fallen trees, the bear gaining ground with every step. No longer did it make sense to count the distance between us in yards. He was feet away.

Mason helped the girls and me over a hip-high tree trunk lying across the path, then got in line in front of Jaime. Alone with my family and with a bear at our backs, the familiar weight of the wilderness we thrived on exerted more than the usual force, and I could feel myself starting to break. Just as when I watched the snowcoach disappear and leave Mom, Dad, Matt, and me alone in the wilderness and when I sold the camera to the entourage, I felt alone. There were people—some of them right there with me and some of them watching—but no one could do anything to help.

"Oh, shit," I whispered in a long, drawn-out sigh.

And then I remembered something important: We were not alone. Isolated, maybe. But not alone.

"God, help us," I whispered in another long, drawn-out sigh.

It had taken me longer than Emma, but like her, I remembered. I didn't need to be afraid. We are never alone. *I* am never alone.

Seconds later, a man came walking up the trail toward us. It was a ranger who, upon seeing us—or, more likely, seeing the bear behind us—unholstered his bear spray. "Did you know he was up there?" he asked when he reached us.

Did we know he was up there? Are you serious? What kind of idiots would follow a bear up there? I was incensed—a feeling that disappeared as soon as I realized his choice to bother with a chastising question meant that we weren't about to die.

"O-o-h n-o-o," I said.

"Is this everyone?" he asked Jaime.

"Yep. This is it."

These were the only words we exchanged with the ranger. The girls walked past him. I walked past him. Jaime and Mason weren't far behind.

Before long, we emerged from the trees and walked toward the parking lot. Emotionally exhausted, I felt as though I'd just thrown myself across a finish line in some kind of twisted race. I wanted to kiss the ground. I looked at my family. Every one of us was alive. No one had been mauled. It was okay, just like our car accident the day before. And I was grateful.

Oohs and ahhs from the crowd gathered at the river signaled the bear had emerged into the open. I turned in time to see him lumber into the river a few hundred feet downstream. We stood among the people paying homage to the bear with their cameras and watched. This was the longest look I got of him. He was a cinnamon black, smaller than a grizzly, but easily mistaken for one because of his color. Still, he weighed several hundred pounds, and—grizzly or not—a bear of that size could maim or even kill with his teeth and claws.

Standing on the edge of the crowd, we learned the bear was the source of the jam we'd skipped when we pulled into the parking lot. When he'd crossed the road to the picnic area, the ranger managing the scene did too. The bear took the path through the woods, and the ranger took the road. By the time he arrived, both our family and the bear had crossed the clifftop. One of the witnesses told the ranger about our predicament, but he didn't immediately head our way. First, he walked down an animal path along the river to clear it of people. Since the river was probably where the bear was headed, that's where he made space. Once that was done, he came for us.

Still stunned, we wandered to the car, climbed in, and sank into our seats, without even the wherewithal to thank the ranger. It was barely past noon, and Jaime and I were ready for a long night's sleep. For that day at least, we were done with the wilderness. Ribbon Lake, the hike we'd planned for later that day, would have to wait. We drove straight to Old Faithful and restored ourselves with the comfort of home and proximity to people on the boardwalk. When evening closed in, we rested our adrenaline-weary bodies and our rumpled souls at the Inn. From our place on the third-floor mezzanine, we relished its subdued soundtrack of quiet conversation mixed with the background percussion of the front door. We relaxed together on the burgundy leather couches with books and games and people-watching.

As sometimes happens at the Inn, a woman asked if she could join the girls on their couch. She chatted as she reviewed her day's photos on her laptop. We learned she was a fellow Iowan, in the park for a Yellowstone Institute class.

She showed us some magnificent photos of a bear. Or perhaps they were average photos of a magnificent bear. She'd been at Sheepeater Cliff that afternoon, learning to do some nature sketching, and had seen "these people and a bear on top of a cliff." She scrolled through photo after photo of the bear, photos which, had we had our wits about us, we could have asked her to email to us.

But we were still stunned, and our wits remained at large. So the bear lives only in our memory. Which is, perhaps, exactly where it belongs.

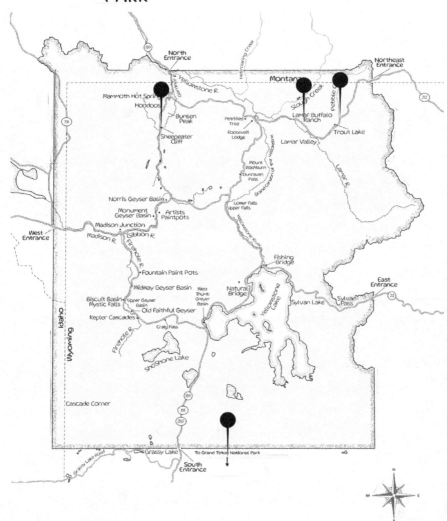

31 NO GUARANTEE

A year later, I headed back to Yellowstone with Dad via the Tetons. It was the same route he, Mom, Matt, and I had taken thirty-two years before, only this time, Mom and Matt weren't with us. Neither were Jaime and the kids. It was just Dad and me.

Our journey took us past String Lake and, as always, we stopped. From the empty parking lot, we made the short pilgrimage through the misty morning's stillness under a canopy of pines adorned with heavy drops from the previous night's rain. An ethereal haze hovered around the boulders jutting from the shallow lake, its glassy surface mirroring the trees, Mount Moran, and the low-lying cloud shrouding its base. We walked to the water's edge, stopping long enough to allow the gentle cadence of the waves breaking against the shore to bring my rushing mind into rhythm with my heart and soul.

When we got back in the van, Dad said, "I hope we don't have to read anything out loud. It wasn't until after I got us all signed up for this workshop that it dawned on me that I was actually going to have to write. You're the writer, not me."

This wasn't entirely accurate. Dad's a technical writer and even a poet, occasionally composing a short verse to commemorate a significant birthday or noteworthy event. He's a writer, just a different kind of writer than me.

"I hope so too," I said. "I haven't read anything I've written out loud since high school."

"I hope the instructor is interested in teaching novices," Dad said.

I nodded. "And I hope the other students are... I don't know... nice."

Five months earlier, he and Mom had attended a Yellowstone Institute Wolf Week at the Lamar Buffalo Ranch.[1] Within an hour of leaving, he'd called to invite me to go back to the ranch with him for a nature writing workshop. That had been in March, when Yellowstone was still in deep winter, and August seemed a long way off. Now it was here, and we both wondered what we had done.

For me that had to do with more than the workshop.

In the descending darkness surrounding our campfire the night before, I'd stared beyond the ring of light and thought about bears. The previous year, one of my life's great what-ifs had become a reality. We'd run into a bear on the trail. We'd also lived—an outcome I did not take lightly. Along with that, I'd learned a little something about the weight of the wilderness that Emma seemed to understand at the age of four: I was not alone. God was always with me. I did not have to be afraid. That didn't mean I wasn't.

After my family and I ran into the bear, rain had fallen for much of the remainder of the week, limiting our ability to get out on the trail. While I was grateful we were confined to the road, I didn't *want* to be grateful we were confined to the road. This was not how I wanted to live—not on the trail and not in my life.

The dangers of wild places were real. After decades of loving

---

1. Like the Yellowstone Association mentioned earlier, the Yellowstone Institute is also part of Yellowstone Forever.

Yellowstone and fearing its wildness, this was something I needed to learn how to navigate.

"Have you seen that sign before?" I asked Dad as we approached the trailhead.

"No," Dad said. "It must be new."

It was new.

During the previous year or two, two deaths occurring in separate incidents prompted park officials to try to get the attention of visitors like me who are as acclimated to the park's bear signs as the bears are to the sound of our bells. Unlike the old signs, which were white with a lot of tiny text and a small picture of a bear, this new one had a block of red, a bold image of a bear, and two short phrases blazed across the top.

BEAR ATTACK:
Are YOU Prepared to Avoid One?

It was eye-catching, different, and in every way disturbing. *What kind of person would voluntarily set foot on a trail marked by this kind of signage?*

Perhaps someone who was prepared.

Layered over the simple but clear depiction of a bear, the sign listed five elements of preparation:

BE ALERT
MAKE NOISE
CARRY BEAR SPRAY
DO NOT HIKE ALONE
DO NOT RUN

It was a sign worded and designed to get hikers' attention. It got mine. I'd spent my life worried and unprepared—on the trail and off.

And while I found it alarming, much more so than Yellowstone's other bear signs, this one answered the questions the others had left me with. It didn't tell me to turn back, but it was clear that encountering a bear was always a possibility and preparation was essential. Line by succinct line, it explained exactly what preparation entailed. Then, below a list of bullet-pointed, all-capped, imperatives of what to do in case of a bear encounter, it slipped in one shocking final sentence: There is no guarantee of your safety in bear country.

No guarantee? That's a fine thing, I thought. I'm a fan of guaranteed outcomes, so risk averse that our insurance agent once mentioned it to Jaime—as if he didn't know. It was obvious: I needed to stick to the road.

Even that isn't a sure deal.

One summer night in 1959, an earthquake shook over half a million square miles, including much of Yellowstone. Its epicenter was near West Yellowstone, Montana, a small community less than an hour from Old Faithful, and its Richter Scale measurement was high enough to wreak a lot of havoc. This included changes in the behavior of thermal features throughout the park, the structural damage that led to the closure of the crow's nest and catwalks at the Old Faithful Inn, and the collapse of a section of road near Mammoth Hot Springs.[2] Near the epicenter, the quake caused the terrain to rearrange itself to the point of creating a new lake.

During our first visit to Yellowstone, Dad drove our family out of the park, through West Yellowstone, and over to the new

---

2. It doesn't take an earthquake to cause a road collapse. The deluge of 2022 washed out several sections of road between Mammoth Hot Springs and Gardiner, Montana. and three more between the Lamar Valley and the Northeast Entrance. I have a photo of Jaime and me standing on one of those now-missing sections, ready to set off on the trail to Trout Lake. Seeing the aerial footage of that stretch of missing road is a weird sensation, indeed.

lake, aptly named Earthquake Lake. Even though its glassy surface and surrounding evergreen forest presented the same serene scenes we'd been seeing all week, to me it felt sinister and foreboding. Sinister or not, once the lake was out of sight, the earthquake was out of mind.

At least, it was out of mind until age and parenthood began reminding me of human frailty and my own mortality. Now, when we approach the area where the road collapsed, I remember. When I hear that someone fell into the Grand Canyon of the Yellowstone, I remember. When I set off on the trail with Jaime and the kids, I remember. There are countless ways to die in Yellowstone.

After the arrival of the new bear sign, I started rereading the old ones. There it was, in bold letters at the bottom of the "bear frequenting area" signs:

THERE IS NO GUARANTEE OF YOUR SAFETY
WHILE HIKING OR CAMPING IN BEAR COUNTRY

How had I missed this? I wondered. It had been there all along.

What's true on the trail is true in life. Just as there is no guarantee of my safety, or that of Jaime's, or our kids, in wild places like Yellowstone, there's no guarantee of safety in the civilized spaces we inhabit every day. I worried there too. Bears of some variety exist everywhere. And we're as likely to encounter one in everyday life as on the trail because life is as untamed as Yellowstone. At least, it's as untamed as Yellowstone should be.

But perhaps safety, or the guarantee of it, isn't the point.

A tamed Yellowstone—smooth, fenced, and safe—would be little more than a drive-through museum, where we could only observe nature from a distance rather than experience it up close. Mom and Dad would never have driven Matt and me across the country for bears behind bars or geysers governed by valves. I never would have taken Jaime. We never would have taken our children. I know this, yet I pave smooth and fence off little parcels of the landscape of my life in a continual effort to guarantee safety, a campaign as naive as my customer's question all those years ago in the Old Faithful Inn gift shop: Where do the rangers keep the animals at night? Because if safety isn't the point, fear isn't the answer.

Mason is all grown up now. He's a math guy, and he tells me the statistics are in our favor, although I know we could still encounter another bear on the trail. And we're certain to face them in the landscape of everyday life.

But if safety isn't the point, and fear isn't the answer, I'm not sure what is.

The next day, Dad and I stopped at the Sheepeater Cliff Picnic Area. We weren't there for a picnic, and certainly not to scramble up the face of the cliff. We were there because Dad wanted to see exactly where we'd run into the bear. He'd been able to envision it, but he wanted to walk through it in person. We took Emma's easy way around the side of the cliff. A few yards beyond the picnic area, the path opened up, revealing a columnar basalt wall curving around a collection of tumbled blocks—an ancient amphitheater in the wilderness.

How did I not know this was here? I wondered as we made our way up to the plateau above the cliff.

I stopped at the edge of the trees. "Here. This is where the bear was when I saw it." Stepping from the cool shade of the forest, we walked into the bright clearing and crossed the cliff. I paused about two-thirds of the way across. "This is about where we climbed up. Mason was over there, alone, across from us in the meadow. And the bear was about seventy-five yards away, where I showed you, coming out of the woods toward us. That's how it started."

As we walked through the late summer grass, I attempted to reconstruct the rest, how Mason had led the way down the hill, the girls and I had followed, and Jaime had stationed himself between us and the bear. Beyond the clifftop, I knew nothing of how we'd come down. There was no trail. I'd simply followed the feet of the people in front of me.

Even as we revisited those terrifying few moments that had happened the last time I'd been at Sheepeater Cliff, it felt comfortable and safe, like home—just like the day we'd run into the bear. And that right there was the problem. A picnic at Sheepeater Cliff followed by a climb up the columnar face felt more like dinner on the deck and a game of frisbee in the yard than a there-is-no-guarantee-of-your-safety event. We felt relaxed, overly so, forgetting about the reality of bears, even though we knew they were there. It's hard to be prepared when you're at that level of ease.

And, just like that, I got it. Safety isn't the point. Fear isn't the answer. Preparation is.

"I don't think we're going to have time for another hike," Dad said as we walked toward the van. We'd lingered at Sheepeater Cliff for too long.

"That's okay. Next time. And maybe next time we can tell everyone we're taking a class and spend the week hiking instead."

He laughed. Just as it seemed logical to attend a Wolf Week class with no knowledge about wolves, enrolling in a nature-writing class implied we might already be able to string words together and have the courage to share them out loud with our classmates. Both Dad and I had our worries, one being that the best part of the week was about to come to an abrupt end.

32 IT CHANGES EVERYTHING

"Natalie!" Randy, the Mammoth Hot Springs Hotel pianist, called across the Map Room. "Do you want to sing?"

Dad and I had stopped to listen to Randy play his original, park-inspired pieces, something our family did every time we visited the park.

Randy was more than a musician, he was also a Yellowstone history buff. What he was really asking was if I wanted to sing an old song titled "Yellowstone," which I did.[1] Recorded in the 1930s by a man who'd worked in the park in the twenties, it's reminiscent of a time when an orchestra provided the soundtrack for an evening at a park lodge. It's an anthem and a love song about Yellowstone and the pull it has on people. As one of those people, singing it in the Map Room makes me feel like part of a historic tradition.

When we first met, Randy asked if I was a singer and, because I'd answered that I was, he asked me to help him close the evening

---

1. As much as I'd love to share the lyrics of this song with you, music copyrights are a complicated thing. A recording from long ago, along with the lyrics, can be found by searching for "Yellowstone" song by Gene Quaw from 1937 on YouTube.

by singing that song. That night, I sang to a nearly empty room. On this day, it was full.

I crossed the Map Room and stood beside Randy, who began to play as the score instructed, slowly and dreamily. After the introduction, I sang, softly at first, until I found my voice. After the final notes faded, it was time for Dad and me to go. Randy hugged me and shook Dad's hand, then we turned toward the van and the unknown awaiting us at the Lamar Buffalo Ranch.

"That was brave," Dad said.

"Oh, thanks. I was a little nervous. Brave will be if I actually read something this week."

For thirty-five years Dad and I had been making pilgrimages to Yellowstone, sometimes together, more often not. Between us, we'd logged more than fifty trips, but when we turned in at the Lamar Buffalo Ranch, it was on a road I'd never been down. A small, orderly settlement set in a wild, expansive landscape, the ranch included a horse corral and a contingent of brown buildings, including an employee residence, a bathhouse, and two cul-de-sacs of cabins.

Before Dad finished parking, a smiling, gray-haired woman walked out of a sizable log structure toward the van. "Are you here for the Yellowstone Institute Class?"

"We are," Dad answered.

"I'm Susan, your program assistant. You must be Dan and Natalie. Bring your food into the bunkhouse and then take the rest of your things to your cabin and get settled. You're in cabin eight. A few of the other students are out on the front porch if you'd like to meet them."

Dad and I carried our food—every uneaten morsel from the previous few days and our provisions for the ones to come—into the bunkhouse. All food at the Lamar Buffalo Ranch had to be stored there. Food odors attract wildlife, and at the ranch, the wildlife in question wasn't bears. It was mice. The park service doesn't want them living in the cabins, and people don't want them moving in and wreaking havoc in their vehicles—something that had happened to some unfortunate soul at the wolf week Mom and Dad attended.

"Well," Dad said when we finished, "we could go out and meet the others."

"We could," I answered, noncommittal. I wanted to start carting our stuff from the back parking lot to our cabin. I did not want to meet anyone new until I had to—preferably at class the next morning.

"We really should go out there. I know you don't want to." Dad looked at me sympathetically. "Your mom wouldn't want to go either."

I sighed, a familial trait I got from him. At forty-four, I still had a thing or two to learn from my dad. "Okay," I said. "You first."

After we established ourselves as non-recluses by meeting three other students, including one who set herself apart as nice by bringing a pan of homemade lasagne all the way from the Bitterroot Mountains five hours away, Dad drove the van to the parking lot behind the cabins. A band of bison spread through the area, some on the lawn, some near Rose Creek along the far side of the main building, and some in the meadow beyond—all of them tearing up mouthfuls of grass. I paused for a moment, pondering the countless bison that once roamed the plains. Then I returned to the task of carrying luggage back and forth from the van.

I'll watch them later, I told myself. I wanted to get settled.

I wasn't gone long, but the bison had drifted off by the time we finished. Disappointed, I had an even more foolish thought than the one that told me I could watch them later: *Tomorrow*. Although I tried to believe it would happen, I knew. Tomorrow is a lie. Wild bison don't show up at the Lamar Buffalo Ranch every evening at dusk. They weren't being rounded up by the rangers.

They were just passing through, and because I was more concerned with my work than with the moment, I had missed it.

The next morning, Dad and I stepped off the pea-gravel path that wound through the settlement. We crossed the bridge, took a seat among the sage near the banks of Rose Creek, and listened. It was our first assignment, observing and recording every sound we heard. We'd met our classmates, some in the kitchen that morning as we'd prepared breakfasts and packed lunches, and others in the classroom. Of the thirteen of us, five were former teachers and four worked in Yellowstone. Our instructor, Dad's primary concern, was a poet—kind, warm, and encouraging.

We relaxed. It was going to be okay.

We boarded the bus after lunch, and Susan drove us down the road and parked in a gravel turnout where we disembarked and filed across a bridge over the Lamar River. Limited only by time and the requirement to remain within Susan's field of vision, we spread through the sage and parked ourselves on boulders and in Crazy Creek chairs throughout the meadow. Our assignment, to observe and describe an organism, seemed simple enough.

I started with the prolific sage. Nothing. I tried again with some lichen, an unusual organism involving a symbiotic union of algae and fungi. Surely I could describe that. Still nothing. I considered the sky. Was a cloud an organism? Probably not. I looked down at the river, hopeful I'd find something there, maybe an otter, a sandhill crane, a bison, or—if I walked down and searched—maybe a trout. A glance upstream revealed two fly fishermen. In the technical sense, they were organisms, organisms that seemed to work for me because—finally—I started to write.

That evening, we walked to an open area farther away from the road to watch the sun set over the Lamar Valley. As it sank, it painted streaks of pink and purple in the clouds that surrounded its molten light—brushstrokes that faded as day disappeared. It was our last official meeting of the day. We were supposed to be observing for sensory details, but mostly people were talking. I was neither observing nor talking. I was focused on the fly fishermen.

When our evening's observation was done, Dad and I sat outside, me in the cabin's standard rough-hewn log chair and Dad in one of the camping chairs that we'd placed on our porch for a moment like this. We listened to the weighty silence of the wilderness night and watched the darkness claim the valley's big sky and sprinkle it with stars. Like the Old Faithful Inn, it felt like home.

The next afternoon, we trekked back to one of the wolf restoration pens. Under Susan's watchful eye, we crossed Rose Creek and hiked into the hills beyond.

"Hey, Bear!" Susan called.

"We've run into a bear over the top of a hill a couple of times," she told us, "and even though we're talking and making noise, I always feel better if I make a little more here."

My anxiety surged.

Then I remembered. I was not alone. Just as I had always taken it on faith that there were bears in the woods even when I didn't see them, I knew by faith that God was with me. He was there when I stood across from the entourage, when Jaime and I faced the bison, and when our family met the bear.

More than that, while there is no guarantee, there is preparation—and we were prepared. We were alert. There were six of us, well over the threshold of three. Several of us were carrying bear spray. We were making noise, and not just noise—extra noise. And every one of us knew not to run.

I did not need to be afraid.

As we crested the final hill, the pen came into view. Nearly an acre in size, its chain-link fence stood a good ten feet tall, with an inward-leaning panel at the top. No one spoke as we walked through a slim opening into the enclosure. Bleached backbones of several large mammals were strewn across the grass. I wondered about their origin. Were they the remains of carcasses fed to the wolves during their acclimation period? Or were they newer than that, animals that happened to have died right there, their bodies picked clean by whatever scavengers happened upon the remains? Around the perimeter, slender doorways opened into smaller pens, places of refuge from the larger group.

The wolf reintroduction was nearly twenty years past, and the pens wore the time. Doors hung askew on their hinges. Young trees were growing inside. On the outside, an old tree had succumbed to the years and fallen on the tall railing, causing it to sag under the weight.

The wolf pens were subject to the same tensions as the surrounding Yellowstone wilderness. Were they to be preserved as they were when the wolves resided there or as they had become over time? *As they were. Obviously.* That was my initial thought, but then I remembered that nothing about Yellowstone—or in life—is as simple as my first reactions lead me to believe. I wanted to bring my children and their children to this place someday, and I knew the broken-down remnants of a chain-link fence wouldn't mean as much as what I saw that day. But neither would a well-maintained, pristine wolf pen. That would be nothing more than a museum. And of all that Yellowstone is, it is not a museum.

The rest of the day unfolded much like the first, with more observations, writing, and reading. Dad joined the class in reading his observations, day poems, and one of his short pieces. I remained silent, not only because I was preoccupied with a particular piece I was writing, but because I was facing a new fear: reading my work out loud.

In the morning we boarded the bus for Pebble Creek, the site of our final wilderness observation. After hiking for a while, we spread out and settled in to write. Dad and I chose boulders along the water's edge, where I listened to the music it made as it danced over the creek's rock-lined bed, noticed the intensity of its emerald moss, and breathed the pine-infused air. Dad took pictures and wandered upstream. Neither of us wrote much.

We both felt a little melancholy. It was almost time to say goodbye to Yellowstone and our week together in the wilderness. When our allotted work time was done, Susan drove us down the road to a picnic area for our last meeting. We gathered together, some of us in our Crazy Creek chairs, some on boulders, and some on the ground. One classmate read. Then another. And another.

"Anyone else?" our poet-instructor asked.

I forced myself to raise my hand, a foreign object stuck fast to an arm that shook to my shoulder.

"A Fly Fisherman," I began. "It was just another hike, to the first meadow at Slough Creek, but it changed everything."[2]

It was true. From those first hikes with my parents and brother where I learned I didn't need to see bears to believe they were there, to the one with Jaime where he decided to try fly fishing, Yellowstone changed my life. Between finding myself snowmobile windshield to nostril with a bison and discovering safety wasn't the point, Yellowstone changed my perspective. And somewhere between that humiliating backcountry fly fishing trip where I learned about following and the terrifying trek across Sheepeater Cliff when I finally understood I was not alone, Yellowstone changed me.

Dad had been right all those years ago. I did like Yellowstone. I was good with people. I did know enough to be able to help park visitors. But what none of us knew was how much influence waking up in Yellowstone would exert—not only over me, but also over Jaime and our kids.

Yellowstone isn't done with me. Whether we're taking a long hike into the backcountry or a short stroll down the boardwalk, the wilderness is still working on me, still changing me, still waking me up.

That's what it's there for, and that's why we keep going back.

---

2. This line, written during this class, became the first words of the first draft of what became this book.

EPILOGUE

These days Jaime and I camp almost exclusively when we visit Yellowstone. We've traded easy access to showers, electricity, and even my beloved Old Faithful Inn for exposure to crisp air, below-freezing nights, and forest on every side. We almost always stay at the Madison campground. Waking each morning with the sun, we make our way to the meadow where the Firehole River mingles with the Gibbon. We wander downstream, our cold fingers wrapped around mugs of hot coffee freshly brewed on our Coleman stove. Before long, we find ourselves walking alongside the Madison—just as Jaime and Mason did all those winters ago.

It's been more than ten years since we ran into that bear at Sheepeater Cliff. Even though we spend more time hiking now than ever, we haven't seen another bear on the trail—up close or in the distance. While I prefer to experience Yellowstone on foot rather than from the road, the reality that there is no guarantee of safety weighs heavily enough that I must regularly remind myself that I am not alone. Jaime and I do our part to be prepared.

Mason, Elyse, and Emma are all grown up and out of the house. They're continuing, each in their own way, the wilderness journey that began when they were young—hiking, sleeping under fabric, camping in isolated campgrounds, backpacking alone in the backcountry. When I'm tempted to worry—and I am—Jaime is quick to remind me that this is how we raised them. Then I remind myself of the truth that they are not alone, which is so much better than my pathetic macaroni and cheese analogy. Because I'm a mom, I go as far as I dare to remind them to be prepared. And because I'm their mom, I celebrate that they go. The wilderness is something they need to experience for themselves.

RESOURCES AND READING

During the four decades that Yellowstone has been part of my life, I have read a lot of books and articles, talked to a lot of rangers, and perused a lot of interpretive boards, maps, websites, and trail guides. I know what I know because I've picked it up from other people along the way, and what I've written here is an outflow of all that accumulated information. In most cases, I don't know when or where I came across specific details, which makes it hard to give credit where credit is due. What I can do, however, is offer a few resources and favorites from my Yellowstone library.

If you're interested in digging a little deeper into some of the specific topics discussed in *Waking Up in the Wilderness*, consider the following books:

Yellowstone Memoirs and Photography

Mountain Time: A Yellowstone Memoir by Paul Schullery

Yellowstone Has Teeth: A memoir of living year-round in the world's first national park by Marjane Ambler

Silence & Solitude: Yellowstone's Winter Wilderness by Tom

Murphy (While all his photography books are a visual feast, this one is my absolute favorite.)

Resources, Guides, and Interesting Reading
Death in Yellowstone: Accidents and Foolhardiness in the First National Park by Lee H. Whittlesey
The Geysers of Yellowstone by T. Scott Bryan
The Guide to Yellowstone Waterfalls and Their Discovery by Paul Rubinstein, Lee H. Whittlesey, and Mike Stevens
Lost in the Yellowstone: Truman Everts's "Thirty-Seven Days of Peril" by Truman Everts (The audiobook makes for good company on a drive to the park.)
The Rise of Wolf 8: Witnessing the Triumph of Yellowstone's Underdog by Rick McIntyre (There are five books in this series. I'm up to book three and each has been a delight, managing to inform while reading like a memoir.)
Yellowstone On Fire! by the staff of the Billings Gazette
Yellowstone Place Names by Lee H. Whittlesey
Yellowstone's Rebirth by Fire: Rising from the Ashes of the 1988 Wildfires by Karen Wildung Reinhart
Yellowstone's Red Summer by Alan and Sandy Carey

Hiking Guides (We consult these every time we plan a visit to the park.)
Day Hikes of Yellowstone National Park Map Guide: The Comprehensive Guide to Day Hikes in Yellowstone National Park by Jake Bramante
A Ranger's Guide to Yellowstone Day Hikes by Robert Anderson and Carol Shively Anderson
Yellowstone Trails: A Hiking Guide by Mark C. Marshall

ACKNOWLEDGEMENTS

One does not write a book without collecting a large contingent of encouragers and helpers along the way. To that end, I offer my heartfelt gratitude to:
- Jody Collins, Megan Gerig, the members of the Marion County Writers Workshop, and the gals in the Wednesday morning Mastermind—each of whom have asked questions, provided critique, and given guidance in various stages of this book.
- The Yellowstone National Park archivists, historians, and interpretive rangers who have answered questions over the years.

Allyson, Angie, Becca, Danielle, Jennifer, Karen, Kathie, Kathy, Linda, and Mom. Your faithful support means so much.
- Rachel, Pamela, Julie, Deb, Libby, and Jenn, each of whom weekly speak into my life—and this project—with encouragement, kindness, creativity, wisdom, and love.
- Earl, Ellie, and Danielle, who encouraged and supported this work from the beginning. Ellie, you were the one who prompted me to start writing this book. Earl, you gave an outdoorsman's perspective and prodded me to get this book out there. Danielle, you've always believed that Yellowstone and this project matter. This book wouldn't be what it is without any of you.
- Lois Flowers, my editor. Thank you for opening the door to friendship by asking to meet *in real life*, for believing in the value of this Yellowstone project, and for helping me shape my words.
- Uncle Brian. I think you nudged me (gently!) in every way you could think of to get this book published.
- Pat and Karen. Parts of this book were written in the still

part of the morning at your place. Thanks for asking the hard questions that helped me figure out what I already knew.

- Mom and Dad, the adventurous stock from which I came. Thank you for heading to workshops and conferences with me and for reading and rereading various drafts of this book. More than that, thank you for driving Matt and me across the country to start us on our own wilderness stories.
- Mason, Elyse, and Emma. You've been great travel companions from the start. Seeing the world through your eyes and watching you experience it with your bent toward enjoying it has challenged me to do the same. Julie and Dion, I appreciate so many things about each of you—not the least of which is your spirit of adventure. We haven't been to Yellowstone together yet, but I hope we get to go—sooner rather than later.
- Jaime. Who knew when we made that first cross-country drive to Yellowstone all those years ago that it would become your place as much as mine and what a through-line it would be in our life's story? Thank you for always believing this book mattered and investing your time and energy in heading into the wilderness with me and the kids. Thanks for van camping and every cup of Madison-brew coffee you've made in the below-freezing temperatures of a mountain morning. There's no one I'd rather wake up in the wilderness with than you.
- You. Thank you for taking the time to head into Yellowstone's wilderness with me by reading this book. Life just isn't the same without travel companions.

take heart & happy trails ~ Natalie

ALSO BY NATALIE OGBOURNE

This is Natalie's first book.

If you'd like to read more from Natalie, please leave a review for *Waking Up in the Wilderness* on Amazon. You can keep up with her on Instagram @natalie_ogbourne or her website—natalieogbourne.com.

Also, just as when she worked at the Old Faithful Inn, she would love to hear about your Yellowstone adventure. Use the contact form on her website to tell her all about your visit to Yellowstone.

ABOUT THE AUTHOR

Natalie Ogbourne is known to some as a "girl who went to Yellowstone and never really came back." A former Yellowstone employee and longtime return visitor, she's been helping visitors plan their time in the park since 1987. She has exactly one athletic bone in her body. It happily divides its time between hiking and downhill skiing. Natalie and her husband enjoy heading into wildernesses of all kinds together and with their grown kids.

Visit Natalie online:
natalieogbourne.com

instagram.com/natalie_ogbourne

Made in the USA
Monee, IL
10 April 2025